Drumming Through Woodsmoke

Poetry and Essays

Jamie Longstreth

*Emily —
Never Stop Creating!
Jamie Longstreth*

Writers Club Press
San Jose New York Lincoln Shanghai

Drumming Through Woodsmoke
Poetry and Essays

All Rights Reserved © 2000 by Jamie L. Longstreth

No part of this book may be reproduced or transmitted in any form or by any means, graphic, electronic, or mechanical, including photocopying, recording, taping, or by any information storage or retrieval system, without the permission in writing from the publisher.

Published by Writers Club Press
an imprint of iUniverse.com, Inc.

For information address:
iUniverse.com, Inc.
620 North 48th Street
Suite 201
Lincoln, NE 68504-3467
www.iuniverse.com

ISBN: 0-595-09539-9

Printed in the United States of America

Dedicated to my daughters Lena and Anna, who brought inspiration, support, and their own unique slant on life to this project.

Contents

Poetry

Blanket on the River 1
Tucking In 3
Awake 5
Winter and the Chill 7
Palate 9
Magnolias 11
Autumn's Promise 13
Ode to a Grove 15
First Fruits 17
Garden 19
Triskadekaphobia 21
Chopin is Unforgiving 23
Dylan 25
Knight 27
Passing Dream 29
Gentle Soul 31
Mary Cries 33

Breaking Free	35
Moon Children	37
Imported Man	39
Iced Coffee	41
Koo-Koo	43
Bearing	45
Port Chicago	47
Come to Earth	49
Dancing	51
Thy Name is Desire	53
Sugar	57
Packing Away	59
"We Aren't in Kansas Any More"	61
Should We Meet	63
Slumber	65
Lessons	67
Saint Valentine's Eve	69
Solitude	71
Seven League Boots	73
Facing the Rest	75
Diamonds in Grey	77
The Persistence of Change	79
The Poet Knows	81
Hope Steals	83
Expensive	85
It's Not Supposed to be This Way	87

Afloat 91
The Vapor of Dreams 93
Creeping Back and Away Again 95

Essays

Hawk 101
Shade 103
Millooneyum Halftime 105
Pondering Y2K 107
Denver 111
Greta and Max 113
1420 Franklin Avenue... 117
729 Ardmore Boulevard 139
The Magic Gift... 155
Holidays Without Non 159
Drumming 163

Acknowledgements

I would like to thank my mother Arlene, who always believed in me. I also thank my family, whose inspiration is beyond value.

My friends and associates on my e-mail lists gave me so much support, praise and assistance. Without them, this project would never have become a reality. Kim, Peter, Doug, Terry, Allen, Don, Marlene, Cher, Mary, and everyone else, you were the first and most important public exposure of my work, and you gave me the courage to do this.

To Candie, David, and Kim, your wonderful energy and hope keeps me alive, thank you.

Introduction

For most of my life, I've been writing. I spent the usual angst filled teenage years writing magical love poems about anyone I fancied. As I matured, I wrote magical angst filled poems about anyone I fancied. I still write magical angst filled poems about anyone I fancy. However, I've expanded into writing about nature, friends, family members, pets, politics, and people I used to fancy. I try to avoid angst. Sometimes it comes out anyway, but that's the finer nature of a poet, to allow people a glimpse into your heart and soul. The magic happens all by itself, if you're fortunate.

I've speculated at length about the finer nature of a writer. Compelled, some might say obsessed, with books, I've had long opportunity. My own writing reflects this compulsion. I go to great lengths to measure up to the best I've read, and most of the time I fail miserably. No matter. The best definition of a writer is one who writes because she has no choice. Not plodding along releasing endless series about fictional worlds, though some of those are fine books indeed. Not working hours on end to meet a publisher's deadline on your latest scheduled release and hating every moment, though there are some very fine writers who are forced to do so. Not writing for bread or board or award, but writing for joy, for pleasure, for life. Writing in the hopes that the magic will happen for you.

I've had a wide range of influence and preference. Dylan Thomas, Alice Walker, John Steinbeck, Ray Bradbury, Salman Rushdie, Robert Heinlein,

Stephen King, Aliester Crowley, Marion Zimmer Bradley, Umberto Eco, heroes one and all. They are my gods of writing. In the old cliché of the lonely poet, the rejected teenager, they were my friends when I had no friends. They were my companions in the desperate and despairing times. They were the magic, and I followed their trail to attempt to place magic into my own work.

Two years ago, my life was more or less settled and solid. I was on a path that led nowhere, but it was a cozy path. When I was cast into a tempest of my own making, I turned from that path and went into deep and frightening woods. I still roam these wild spaces, but I have made them my own and found safe places where I can rest. Writing is one such place. Someone once told me "Despair breeds good poetry". I'd rather have the good poetry without the despair, but I don't suppose I can have it both ways. I venture into those woods now with relish, even into the scariest bramble patches, because I know what riches hide out of the light, like rare and delicious mushrooms, waiting for one with the patience and persistence to seek them out. I feared the feelings that led to these treasures. Having dwelt in this sometimes-dank forest for so long, I no longer fear. Not always, anyway.

Enjoy the journey through my woods, and fear not. It is safe here, and the paths are, finally, well marked.

Poetry

Blanket on the River

Shiver beneath the blanket
As you flow on, and I invade you
Where light pervades, I protect
And invade and seek to become you
And have you become me, one.

Tremble and carry on as if
I don't exist but
Where is the air? It's not here
It's there on the other side of me
Imagine you're safe, persist.

The life within you slowly
Slows and dies but
Will arise again when
The light returns and the
Air warms and the blooms wash
Past in springtime skies.

For now I will play
This subtle game with
Wool of chill and frost
Above your vein, the same.
But covered and hidden
I'll allow you to remain.

Tucking In

And now beneath
The new fallen flakes
They insulate me tight
Against you, disguising your might
And mine, alike.

You are warm
Moving beneath my grasp
And I form, your skin
In sheets, piecing together
And solid again.

The white feathers waft
Onto me and take the sunlight
Cast it back into the blue
Its warmth unwanted here
And I form anew.

A jigsaw molded
With the newfallen down
You are mine, no matter
The escaping over the dam
You flow beneath me, again.
Succumbing without a sound.

And I hold you safe and dead
Under me, under the frost
Under the snow, you flow
And I go on, relentless
Your safety, I confess
Held in icy tendrils like a loving moss.

Awake

No, not this triumph
The groaning creaking
And you are victorious
Your ally, the sun and its breaking
And I break, slow, and flow
Atop you, warm again.

The sweet singing
Of the season, not here yet
But nearing, collecting its debt
Of ice and cold
And snow, melted,
In its fiery glow.

For now, I allow you
This victory, this dance
As you cavort and I collapse
Shuddering downstream
Joining you, and your dream.

Your rebirth is my demise
I blend and leave you
Though I never leave.
My essence, your lives
And yours, mine, eternally.

Winter and the Chill

Winter and the chill it brings
Steals over my heart like a strange fog
I seek out the light before, and
I hear the pealing of the bell ashore
I cannot see it yet; my eyes will not open.

So I struggle blind against the currents,
The chill fog freezes my psyche.
The frost kissed panes of my reality
Listen, listening for the song of hope.
It chimes, dimly, somewhere in the harbor.

Winter follows hard after fall,
And the memories of blossom remain
Pensive recollections, and wonder,
Wonder shall they ever return.
And know that if they do, it will be a new flower.

For the blooms killed
In winter are never to be reborn, and so
I fear that is for the best. Sleeping,
I drown again in the winter's chill
Awaiting the uncloaking of springtime.

Shall the fog roll away from my spirit?
No, warmth is not for today,
But a dim reminder of another season.
In the faint promise, the frost remains
Etched with its own barren flowers.

 Palate

The hillside stark with granite
With bare wood, dank fallen leaves
Decay, warming the ground
Hiding the life
A sleeping easel

Then all at once, a brush stroke.
A hint so subtle it seems illusion
A shadow of a guess of a memory
Topping a lone tree.

Perhaps it's white, or orange, or red
A faded remembrance of fall's blaze
Until it becomes
A promise fulfilled

Then another, and another still
The reds and oranges and whites
Become a blur of living green
As the hillside explodes into vibrant spring

From undergrowth to limbs questing for sky
Green spreads over the canvas
Like an artist gone mad with a strange fever
Until it is covered.

And the miracle of that single brush stroke
Is hidden
And forgotten
Until next spring.

Magnolias

Misplaced southern belles
Scream in opulent pink
Assaulting the eyes, brash
Wondering in their finery
What brought them to the hell
Of this cold place, they shrink
And shiver, and thrash
The first blooms of spring
Poor cold imported things.
Indignantly they fade so quickly
Their skirts drop around them
And embarrassed, they shirk
Trembling and nude
Then they are thin
Pretending it's only a quirk
As the green emerges, a saving grace
They smile with complacent face
The south will rise again
In the leaves that warm
While they dream of home
And a julep sipped, telling the story
The moldering crushed petals remain
Of the magnolia's fallen glory.

Autumn's Promise

The patchwork blanket lies over the hills
Warmth and safety against the cold
The trees quilt it for the earth
With the final blaze of summer's life.

Brilliant hues of gold and red
And all the colors in between
Fall like threads to the drowsy ground
And weave them into coverlets

The chill earth in winter's sleep
Beneath the blanket scattered there
Will take its warmth and fade the leaves
And bring the hues back to life in spring

The reds and golds of autumn's joy
Give us a final glimpse inside
The life of what we see each day
And hardly notice 'til it's done.

A fond goodbye to summer's life
And off to sleep with what's beneath
Now white and grey is all we'll have
'Til the promise is fulfilled in spring

The leaves release their gaudy tones
And slow through winter fade away
They feed the earth 'til brown and pale
And warm the sleeping infant seeds

The promise autumn makes to us
Is never broken, never betrayed
The reds and golds of the patchwork quilt
Flower upon the trees in spring

Ode to a Grove

Sleep cool in majesty
With your huddled ancient wisdom
Watching
Watching the young ones reach out
For the first sun of midwinter
They send buds, gleefully
Rejoice singing then flinching back
As the tight fingers of frost
Pinch them
They will learn.
They are not yet wise
Their youth is betrayed by the pain
While you stand still and comforted
Restless and sad
Wanting and wary
Remembering your youth
When you reached out, anxious for that
First sun of midwinter
And cried when merciless frost bit
And killed the most tender part of you
The most precious part of you
You learned caution.
But sometimes you envy the sapling youth

The reckless spontaneity
That allows them to take chances
And bloom
Gloried
If only for a day.

First Fruits

Summer peaks in glorious heat
Blooms rot and drop
And make fruit
First fruits, reap what you sow.

Tended loving or abandoned
To their own devices
Corrupt seed breeds corruption
Getting back what was given

Abandoned to fertility,
I'm hacking through weeds
To find the sweet flowers
And smell their passionate dreams

The growth too thick,
No time to harvest
Just to glance the potential
Of the bursting rain-cracked skins

Reap what you sow
Again, promise not to neglect
And know all the while
The row is too long, and the hoe too blunt.

 Garden

Neglected so long
A garden chokes 'neath the weeds
Hungry greedy things that they are
Strangling the good
Drown the light, clog the soil
The garden sleeps and nearly dies.

Tenacious, the flowers
Sleep and wait, knowing
They will be tended again
Or else the seeds
Will be borne away by the wind
Or the birds.

Hearts are gardens
Where despair is a weed and
Pain is a choking vine and
They choke the light of love from
The beauty and hope that
Live deep within.

The heart slowly dies
'Til you tend it again
And pull the pain and despair

*And anger and fear away from
The blooms, the blooms that can
Once again thrive.*

*Freed and open again the
Beauty and peace of the heart
Grows into a wonderful sanctuary
Where you dwell, and hope
To again invite love inside
To feel peace there.*

*The seeds of a heart
Are sown deep into a life
To be borne away by the wind
Of a smile or by the
Flight of a kiss or the
Caress of a lover.*

*Never dying only sleeping
Choked by weeds but somehow
Living deep deep inside
Waiting for the patient and loving
Hand of one willing
To tend it into bloom once more.*

Triskadekaphobia

No luck today, but I'm not sad,
Seems my luck lately has all been bad.
It's been that way now for a while,
Sometimes each day is an unending trial.

I happened to notice something today,
A revelation in the strangest way!
That sweet black cat that crossed my path
Is actually white, and in need of a bath.

Is it all a question of perception?
And the fragile mind's kind deception?
That luck is about, be it good or bad,
And the view is skewed as to what we have had?

I've broken mirrors 'til I lost track
And walked under ladders' folded backs
And now I gaze at my reflection
In pieces, angled fly-eyed detection.

See, the snake-eyed dice are in my hand
And luck is something I have planned.
My fate is mine to keep or change,
It matters not if that seems strange.

For this is mine to make the best
And put my dreams out to the test.
Today, the thirteenth, a Friday morn,
My luck in life will be reborn.

Chopin is Unforgiving

I neglected him too long,
His notes are an accusation
I sit and fumble over the keys
Again and again
Searching for the magic I once knew
But it has gone

I curse myself for this neglect
My Fredrick, my dream
The notes I cannot reach with
Inadequate fingers, impossible tenths
Searching for the memory within the joints
But it has gone away

So again I am an infant
Before this vision of ivory and
Carved cherry wood that taunts me
Reminding me of the overtones
I search for the ease with which I once played
But it hides from me

The valse brilliante is clear in my mind
The notes cascading from the
Fingers of one who once knew the

Secrets of their birth and their life and their death
I seek the secrets out once more
And swear not to neglect them again

Slowly he returns to me
In the company of other dead men
That live on in the ether of sound
The echoes of his dream flowing through clumsy hands
I reach for them and grasp them to my heart
And taste again the beauty of his mind.

Dylan

Words wrapping across other words
Calling still more to their side
Incredulous, grasping for understanding
Struggling, unblocking meaning within
The flowing meter and constricted rhyme
Subtle insidious twining round the purpose

Meaning there and gone and changing
Twisting with each reading
Clarity flees then returns
Smelling of the salt of the Welsh seaside
That bore him and his demons
Sea breezes that sent words and worms and madness

Thirty-seven years before I knew
Hundreds of poems flew from my pen
I never knew him and glad I didn't
Youth's insecurity would have fled before such power
Maturity enables understanding
Of the difference in expression, and acceptance

Dylan, tortured, tempted and transcending
The time and circumstance that gifted you
And left you to die too soon

*Your life words poems stories plays
Live to inspire the persistent and
Discourage the inadequate*

*I've yet to learn where I fall
The nerve of me to write of him
One so blessed and cursed
Holding magic that molded words like clay
While I merely fumble, my words mud pies
In the hands of a poetic child.*

Knight

Standing along a chill coast fog enshrouded
His armor gleams dully in the half-light
Knight brave and dear
Searches through his helm for nothing
And everything

Strong knight alone in the mist
Mounted on the steed of his dreams
The beast is huge but insubstantial
And ever changing, hues fade and chase
Across it, and return again

White knight tinged in gray
Questing ever after the dragon
Of his pain and the grail of his joy
And the castle of his sanity, where he can
Nurture the dreams into substance

Holding himself straight and confident
The curve of his mouth merry
The light in his eye bright and true
The burden of his hurt rests heavy on the
Steed, yet on and on he quests

The faith is in his eyes as he gazes
Ever westward, searching for something...

He knows not what he seeks.
A vision upon the water to guide his
Dream, beckoning to his heart.

Dear Knight, turning the steed and
Renewing the quest, his dream
Revived by the hand outstretched on the
Waves, the sense that he will be
Fulfilled if he but believes in his vision

I watch him go from across the water
My hand and my heart open and
Pour strength and hope and whatever
Slim guidance I can offer, as he rides into
The new day with a blessing on his strong shoulders

Riding along a chill coast as morning opens
His armor shining in the newborn sun
Knight brave and dear
Searches through his helm for nothing
And everything.

Passing Dream

There once was a knight
With dented armor and a rusted sword.
His quest forgotten, he roamed the land
Asking far and wide for dragons
Or griffins, or damsels in distress
When none were apparent, he invented them
Embraced them, and then conquered them.

The dragons breathed their fire upon him
And the griffin's razor talons scraped the rust
From his shield and his sword.
The damsels and their fine linen
Cleaned the armor of the smoldering dragon soot
Leaving it gleaming, like his eyes.
And on and on he went

Still questing after his mission.
His journey never ending.
Being a kind and fair knight,
Of gentle birth and disposition
He believed the best of the travelers he met
Along the pitted, twisted road
And helped them when he could, with a smile.

And as the knight in newly gleaming armor
Looked to the sky, he saw a shape,

A phantom shadow twisted like a bird
And like a rose, and like a daydream
The wings of the shadow hid the thorns,
And the tears that fell from the face
That fought to stay behind the mist.

Pride in the knight's spirit lit the mist from within
Reflected back into the face of the sun
The presence there smiled with a tear
As a worn and tired hand began to reach out
Then stopped, just short of revelation
And drifted back into the westward winds
On the currents of sorrowful joy in his growth.

Brave knight, brave dream
Passed from the reality of imagination
Into the shadows of fond remembrance
As his steed grew more real, and strong
Able to carry him and his realization
His dreams come to birth, at last
And another's gone to rest.

Gentle Soul

*Gentle Soul, what is it behind your eyes
What hides under the laughter?
What depths lay buried in your sad smile
And how do you find your answers?*

*Shall I weave you a story
Of love's unending tempest?
Or sing you a sweet melody
Of the joy I see in your reflection?*

*Gentle soul, my sweet sad companion
We walk hand in hand through fire
And laugh at the sadness that licks at our heels
Ever concealing our crying*

*Shall I sing you my dream?
The one that you inspired?
Or build you a bridge of words,
To bring you to rest at my side?*

*Gentle soul, the twin of my heart
I embrace you ever in my mind
And carry the image of your sad gentle eyes
'Til the day that your hand rests in mine.*

Mary Cries

Her eyes fill with tears
As she fights with her will
The battle of emotion
To have her words heard
Her loss acknowledged
Her pain not in vain, but to an end.
An end that will save other mothers
Other wives
The same tears.

Mary cries for her child
For the needless loss
For the beauty of a rose
Plucked from life before reaching full bud

She fights, remembering
The ache in her heart remains
But she bravely puts it aside
To help other mothers, other wives
Avoid the tears she shed, and sheds still.
Pushing for reform
For justification, and perhaps
For someone to tell her,
"Mary, I am sorry your child died."

Mary cries for her child
For the loss of her love
Of her life's flower
Uprooted before it could grow to completion.

She lives as best she can
The shade of her child and her husband
Dead too, from a broken heart
Standing at her shoulders
She works too hard, too long
As she tries to send them to heaven
Where they already sing with the angels.
But she can only feel them at her side.

Mary cries for her life
For the loss of her dreams
The waste of her most loving labor
Snatched from her by uncaring hands.

Breaking Free

His limbs grow weary from the pressure of the days
They hold so much, so long, so strong
His pain is a settled part of his life
Been there so long he hardly notices
But for the dull ache in his soul where his life was

He longs to tear away from the soil
That holds him tight to the ground
The same place that gave him birth clinging
To the soles of his feet and rooting him
He sighs, and awaits a sign from the seasons.

A wind arises and tugs at his heart again
He smells the breeze and the promise it holds
A new beginning and a sad sad ending
A dream denied and life rising anew
He feels the ground loosen beneath his feet.

Closing his eyes as the tears water his spirit
He feels the wounds closing at last
The blood in his veins ready to carry healing
And rebirth to his heart, to his mind, to his soul
He tears his roots from the ground

Walking free and alone and unsure now
He grows stronger with each stride
Gathering speed and shedding burdens
Along the way, he looks up into the healing sun
And smiles again at the new dawn.

Moon Children

I can feel it from here.
The call of the game, hide and seek.
And three enchanted children laughing.
I'm laughing with them.

I can feel their wonder.
As they watch and wait and marvel at the spectacle
The lady covered in a cloth of night
Coyly, teasing them with final glances.

How I wish I were there!
To join with the bright sparkle of their young eyes
And share the moment of revelation
As she peeks out the other side.

Her bright countenance blessing them.
These stars fallen to earth
She tells them she was only playing
Eternal, the light returns to her face.

And they will rejoice
As the veil falls away from her beacon
I am a moon child with them
And sing great praise to her return.

Imported Man

California man came a long way
To be where he sits
In his white wrinkled shirt
And sandals...Guitar in hand
Playing a song of happiness
Sad tinged, missing a taste
Perhaps the chill mists
Over afternoon tea
Perhaps something simpler still
The entranced eyes gazing
Over the cup at breakfast,
And he pets his cat, dreaming.

Where do his dreams take him?
Over mountains and oceans
Forward and back again
To a past unyielding and a future
Unknown to all, but in his hands.
Wistfully gazing over distant lands
In his imagination's eye
And living today, playing his heart
Over the strings, six at a time.
Giving all he can with tune and time
And realizing all his schemes
Within a stave of five lines, four spaces.

*All in good time, for the imported man
4/4 or cut in half, beating like his heart
Good and strong but still delicate
Delightful and tender the melody
Guarded in a wry grin,
The hurt disguised in a happy tune,
Yet tinged dark just enough to show
The import of the feelings
California's home, but a long way
From where his dreams live
Along the sharp flats of a terrain known
To none but the imported man.*

Iced Coffee

Taste takes me back
Nut brown and tingling
Tongue exploding with cool spicy
Coffee and chicory
In the thick crystal glass with the metal band around the rim
The flowing letter F emblazoned
And condensation running onto my palms
As I begged a sip
The coldest thing I ever tasted.
Eight years old
The forbidden savor of coffee
Mixed with the exclamation of ice cubes
Clinking in the glass, merry.
Non never refused me the taste
The sip of stimulating cold
Knowing nothing refreshed like it.
No taint of sugar or cream
Only a lifelong love of the taste
A lifetime's memory of the feeling
Of the cool kitchen where I held the glass
Scared I might drop it
But understanding the joy of the taste
Was worth the risk
And that I'd be forgiven, anyway.

Koo-Koo

A thousand verses have been written
About kittens
And their cunning cuteness
The way they cuddle and purr,
But none were about mine, before.

Can I say something new
About the fluff ball bounding round the house?
The sweet mews,
And the way he kisses my chin?
Nothing new therein.

Kittens are a tiring topic
For poets round the sphere
And nothing new to hear
Nothing can be said that hasn't been clichéd
Told over again in a thousand precious ways

So I shan't write a verse about my kit,
And the teeny teeth that bit.
For it's an old subject, true.
No matter that he is sweet,
I'd rather be discreet.

No words on the huge blue grey eyes
Or the tiny kitty cries
Of "Hello, I missed you" upon my return.

Not a mention of relearning
To wear jeans and shoes as well,
Until he learns to control the claws from hell.

No prosaic phrases on the quest for his tail.
And how he never fails
To beg, starving, for my dinner plate.

No, I won't talk of his gait
As he leaps about the house,
Chasing the dog as if he were a mouse.

Because, a thousand verses have been written
About kittens
And their cunning cuteness
And the way they cuddle and purr
(But none were about mine, before.)

Bearing

I, with others, help bear her to her grave
Remembering the touch of her soft hand.
Given to comfort,
Or to console.

She held me when I was small, and she seemed tall.
Took my hand to cross the street
To board the bus
To enter the church.

Then I grew tall, and she was small
I took her hand to help her into the car
Up the stairs
Down the hall.

She was frail and weak, shrunken
But her character was enormous
Even taller than I was,
And I stood head and shoulders above her.

But the size of her spirit dwarfed me
And the scope of her faith was boundless
Larger than the church
And deeper than the sacred mysteries.

*Now she lies enclosed in steel and satin.
My share of the burden seems so little,
When she carried us all upon her small shoulders,
Holding them straight and proud.*

*I, with others, hold myself straight and proud.
The last time I will help her through a door,
Up the stairs,
Into the church.*

Port Chicago

The voices from long ago
Fifty years ago, they fought
Though they weren't allowed to fight
They did what they were permitted, as men of color
To serve their country.

They were lied to.
No detonators, they said
It won't blow up, they said
The white officers assured the men
While wagering on the speed of their crews
And laughing behind their hands at the ignorance there.

One shell sent down the ramp
Too fast, too hard, who knows?
Three hundred thirty seven men died
When the ships blew up.
Three hundred or more injured, mutilated, blinded.
Frightened, betrayed.

A week in the hospital, and a column is formed
They march to their assignment
Left, left, left right left
Column Left, and to the docks

Back to the ships
Back to the danger and death.
Some were brave enough to refuse.

Trembling, they faced their officers
And a charge of mutiny
Unarmed mutiny, shipless mutiny.
Silent peaceful frightened mutiny.
Guilty as charged, and hard labor.

Fifty years later, they remain betrayed
Five old men speak of their pain
And the charges that were never erased
And the shame that should never have been
And the lives that were lost even as they lived.
Betrayed again.

Silence is all that greets the questions
About what happened at Port Chicago.
To the shame, now, of those that condemned men
To labor because they did not wish to die
Senselessly
Stateside
They understood they were thought expendable.
And all they wanted was to serve.

Come to Earth

No more the cerebral wanderings
And the clasping of words.
No more higher purpose,
We are not above this,
Set high in this transcended plain.

No more caressing with thought,
Wrapping the sterile comfort of synapse
Around each other.
No more the thrust of ideas probing,
Penetrating, flowing together.

There is a need for stripped and
Seething contact of flesh.
The power of scent and touch and flavor.
The sweat of passion and joy
As bodies commingle.

Take me from this high shelf,
Else climb up here beside me.
Allow me to sense the quiver and pulse
Of your flesh as I guide you to earth,
And both of us to heaven.

No more this platonic ideal of a dream
I am woman, and call touch to me.
Raw and fertile and rich with passion,
Feel my need and make it yours
As words lose purpose, and you fill my soul.

Dancing

The words weave round
In a minuet, paced carefully
Glancing coy,
Keeping space
Shy smiles,
Distanced invitations.
Come into my arms
But not too close
Don't think too hard
What the feeling would be
It might be intolerable
The longing once more
Refreshing past hurts
The wounds too open
Dance with me
But not too intent
Keep that space in
Your sweet concentration
Perspective buffers
The ironic smiles
Disguising the craving
For a tender gaze.
Measured steps
Caution still in my hand
Not ready to release it

A dove into the dream sky
To meet another
And dance there
Uninhibited in the
Ethereal space between minds.

Thy Name is Desire

From the wand'rings of a vacant heart
I sought one that would first listen
As I ever listened
And then, would want.
As I ever wanted.

In the trav'lings of a wounded spirit
I longed for one to start me healing
And vanquish the injuries
Inflicted by the dragon's fire
The scars that refused to fade.

Then I spied another roaming the same
The blasted terrain of treacherous love
Clutching at wounds bought
With the high price of devotion
And bandaged with a wry gauze.

In the laughter from his mouth
I recognized my own cynicism
And my own hope in spite of all
So I spoke to the traveler
In tones not too filled with longing.

He answered with his own cynicism
His own kindness, as well

I saw a wounded spirit like to mine
And smiled inside
But kept my own counsel.

'Twas a long talk we had
The wanderer and I, on that plain
And around us flowers bloomed
And grass grew green
And the sun shone through the mists.

I gazed into his generous heart
Looking for his name
Seeking through the open spirit there
At last, saw it gleaming
Like a freshet through a serene wood.

Into the eyes of the stranger
I deigned to look
And casting my voice low
Spoke to him, keeping my hope locked away.
"Thy name is desire"

"Hast thou come for me
In the wasteland of ruined dreams?
And how shall we proceed?

Healing, or asking to heal?
Wanting, or wary of want?"

He spoke not, only took my hand
And smiled a lovely smile
Leading me into a longing dream
I know not how it ends, only that
The name of that dream is desire.

Sugar

Love sweet, so sweet the taste of it stays
For weeks of days and years of weeks
While I re-invent and augment
And try to persevere, intact, while crumbling
A rock candy sculpture in a driving rainstorm.

Gluing the sand castle together
With strands of honey, watching the battlements fall
Against the waves. Relentless weather
Of truth erodes the face
And I cling to the embrace, valiant.

Struggling for understanding, acceptance
Filling pail after pail with rationalization
Ghostly sweet sensation fades after all
And I remember your touch, a silken strand
As I stand, a breakwater against the storm,
Melting.

Packing Away

As you move away from me
A piece at a time, I try to help
Taking the pieces of you that you left
In my heart,
Looking at them, remembering, and packing them away.

Ever treasured, the mementos
The smiles and jokes and musings
Understood so well, incomprehensible to others
Like twin minds,
Reunited for a short time then parted.

A crystalline laugh, delicate and rare
Goes into a tissue of memory, careful
Preserved to look at again and again
Not with sadness
But with the pensive knowledge that none will see the like.

Porcelain figurines of desire,
The fine work of delicate paint on their faces
Some smile, some bear the tracing of tears
Setting a theme
Recollections for both of us, but remaining in my care.

Photographs framed with the mist of understanding
And unfulfilled half formed dreams

The possibilities never really explored,
They already fade
I take them out of the light to preserve their beauty.

A melody tinkles from a music box
And the words dance like marionettes atop
The magic of that moment undiminished by time
Fresh and clear
I listen once more, then put it aside to live in my dreams.

A box at a time, a longing glances, as they are stored
And stacked and carefully numbered
Among the things I treasure most in my life
And in my heart, now
They succumb to the reasonable priorities of reality.

"We Aren't in Kansas Any More"

Kansas of the heart
Dull and dry, an arid waste
With sepia toned memory
Fading to a lingering taste
That's ended before it starts

Again and again
Chasing the cyclone
Throwing caution to the wind
Watching my dreams swirl
As the dust settles and I'm alone.

Where is the color?
That Technicolor world
When I peek out the door
The leaves are supposed to unfurl
Into hues of wonders in store.

The only thing that greets me
In the door's dour frame
Is more dust and wind
Another helping of pain
And sepia's all I can see.

*So off to dream again
Of magenta flowers, fields
Of green and gold,
As caution goes flying with the wind
Once again, before my heart goes cold.*

Should We Meet

Should we meet in fall's ginger spiced teardrops of leaf
Cozying against the onrush of winter, lying in wait
Beyond the sunshine that fires the trees
The air mulled with autumn spice
As our eyes meet again for the first time

Should we meet in summer's merciless and merry kiln
Scorched dry and longing for drink
Pavement baking in the relentless heat
The fire that is would be born anew
As our fingers brush together like grasses seeking a familiar breeze

Should we meet in winter's icy embrace
Clean and sleeping and in wait for release
Seeking the frozen firefly of a compassionate heart
To free the wastes of chilled complacency
As we become snow warmed children, once more frolicking against the gale

Should we meet in the birth of spring
While the land erupts in exuberance
And riots of blooms land soft at our feet
Glorying in newfound fertility of love and laughter
As we twine together at last, in a happy disbelief.

Should we meet, at all, my sweet.
Should I learn that you live in this lifetime
Any season would be fitting
For the roots of our hearts are deep and entwined
In the wheel of the earth, and ever have been.

Slumber

In a sweet slumber she sees him
And the promise in his eyes
Mystery solved at last, yes.
What she believed was true
In sweet slumber.

His arms 'round her warm
And all feels right as summer rain
Soaking herself in his touch
The promise of his kiss
Brings heart storm thunder again.

Chill in the air, this dream holds
And heat in the heart and body
No confusion, only clarity
Like a message,
Or a book read shoulder to shoulder.

The script is pleasing
And promising, like tree buds bursting
His neck warm against her mouth
His breath like springtime wanting
Clicking into place, a puzzle solved.

She knew him of old and of new
And met him again, in slumber
When she woke at last from her voyage
She tasted his lips, sweet wine
Smiling at sweet slumber's gift.

Lessons

Living with the pain and wonder of love
You learn some things if you're wise
But I'm not wise.

I've got a friend that isn't too wise either.
He goes off over and over
Giving his all and glorying in the sensation of love
And hurting all over again

He's a sweet guy, but a little too sensitive
I tell him
Baby, you have to learn a little self-preservation.
I thought no one was worse than me,
But you take the cake
For wearing your heart on your sleeve.

He sings to his wonder and pain
Learning, but ignoring the lessons given
He's wise enough to try to love again

Guess I could learn from that.
But I can't, it hurts too much
I glory as much as I can, feeling ashamed
And afraid, a little, to give all with abandon

I'm a nice lady, but a little too jaded
People tell me
Baby, you have to learn to live a little
It's not always a mistake
To wear your heart on your sleeve.

So, I keep trying to trust
But there's always a place that stays
Safe and locked up tight

Watching the fools fall in love
And laughing behind my hands
But envying them all the same
Wishing I could let go that much.

It's a mean old world
I can see it
But you have to learn to take chances sometimes
Because a heart's meant to be shared
Not sheltered in a cold cave of fear.

Saint Valentine's Eve

With hope in my eyes
And a dream in my heart
I heard your voice, saying
Place a candle in the window for me.
Make a light for my arrival at your door
And the realization of our dreams.

So I set a dozen candles or more
On the porch
On the stairs
In the window
And they all dimmed beside the light in my heart
Shining bright enough to burn.

Thus I sat, and waited for you
The music carefully chosen
Checking makeup over and over
Pulling nervous wrinkles out of clothes
Making more wrinkles
My heart beating sure and strong and joyous.

My faith in you, complete
Trusting you with my entire existence
Which I had placed into your hands

A month or more before
Then, a still moment of serenity,
When I realized an important fact.

In the light of the candles
There lived a perfect moment of happiness
And no matter what the future held
That would never change.
Though my dreams did not survive
That moment did, and ever will.

Older, wiser now
More cautious, and withdrawn
I light fewer candles
And that which burned in my heart
Now waits, guarded
For a moment that lasts more than an hour.

Solitude

*The wisdom of solitude
Teaches one to listen deep
To the music of the soul
To decipher its most secret need.*

*Many lessons can be learned
If the state is not bemoaned
No companion sought, but
Solace found in being alone*

*Do not forsake the gift
Of the time to quest the heart
Treasures unknown may come to light
As a new awakening starts*

Seven League Boots

Sweet, sweet, the words I read,
Coming from your fingertips to my eyes,
Like tender kisses with thinly veiled lust,
And I return your meaning to you,
Doubled and redoubled yet again,
Sweetened by my kiss,
And salt with my own desire.

And so I don these seven league boots
To bridge the distance
Between our worlds
I'll lay beside you in your dream
Your breath will be my kiss,
And mine yours, tender
In the ether that divides us.

And when you awake,
The mist and shadow that slips from your arms
Will be my memory
As I place the boots on my feet
And steal away to my reality
Leaving you to yours
Until the next journey brings me to your side.

Facing the Rest

Now in a rush comes the rest
What's lead to this point? Mistakes,
So the assumption stated.
But let us embrace the change,
And leave the future undebated.

Ever more complex, the threads
Of life weave round,
Gossamer tendrils reach the ground
And stream to the sky ahead
Leaving one perplexed, wondering.

So one must stand tall, confident
And brave against the rushing waves
Even if the precipice begs a fall
And despair screams to cling
To what can be again, saved.

To close one's eyes
And dive headlong into the unseen
Is bravery at its most divine
Foolhardy, but trusting the song
Echoing in your ears, that craving keen.

*The path is unlit but for faith's beam
And the journey begins, once again
Through the forest dark and deep
And frightening, wends this trail, this current
This life that somehow will not fail.*

Diamonds in Grey

So much we can see
If we only look deeper

Concentrating on the smaller aspects
Of our lives
And losing the beauty of the whole.
Seeking clarity and thus missing
The grace of the blend

Our lives sparkling diamonds
Twinkling beyond our perception
As we examine the facets one by one
Searching out the flaws
Seeking the imperfections

Forcing our vision toward black and white
Not realizing that all the rainbow
Is contained inside our shades of grey,
It's all too easy to miss the point.
To miss the powerful beauty of sad colors

The sparkle in a child's eyes
And the glistening of a tear
The look into a ballroom mirror
And the shattered panes of our heart
All part of the same beauty

The sky's brilliant blue
Under the murkiness of the storm clouds
And the vibrant fall shades
Fading to brown, but returning
In the rebirth of springs bloom

All contained in our grays
All one in the clear
And imperfect cut
Of our lives

If we'd only step back
And see it as one.

The Persistence of Change

Dependable world set in complacency
We sit smug and secure in the surety
That some things are eternal and constant
We'll be warned of anything momentous
And can prevent the overtly monstrous.

Not so, this ingrained insistence
How precious the human persistence
Our belief of unchanging security
Of the little place we make for ourselves
The impossibility of random eruption.

So childlike in the unshakable faith
And the unquavering standard held straight
Our desire for constant assurance
And our fear of anything perplexing
We are so sweetly incurably inflexible.

Deny it if you will my darlings
But humans have rarely the daring
To stare change in the face with all bravery
And dare it to make us irascible
And send us off upon the unfathomable.

One asks to take change in installments
Set schedules that are easily handled
But the shock of the ultimate intrusion
Of the change, so daringly persistent
Is the constant of human existence.

The Poet Knows

When the muse sleeps
The poet knows
Though the human rarely understands

The words that once fell
Like rain on the parched heart
Have for a time dried and left tracings

Sweet, droplets upon the page
Upon the eyes
Words fallen from the mind of the heart

The salt-rimed memory
Of the prolific words
Stays with the poet in the heart of his mind

But the poet knows
To rest and to wait
And let the muse have her leisure

For she is a kind mistress
If indulged
And will always return

If you keep her place
By the hearth of your soul
Warm and waiting for her.

Hope Steals

Hope steals in on gossamer wings,
Bearing the promise of beginnings
And endings,
And the revelation that none are forthcoming.

Hope cheats at dice, hers are loaded.
The seven-come-eleven and
Baby needs a new pair of shoes,
Poor baby, unshod chillblained feet.

Hope is a fantasy dressed in rags
Promising beauty under the tawdry cloth.
The promise is a lie.
The cloths hide sores, rotten with depravity.

Hope steals ambition's energy
When the truth is unveiled,
The lie revealed
To be all the reality there is.

Hope springs eternal
Then laughs, screeching siren of insanity.
Twining round the feet
And leaving the smell of rot.

Hope steals in on gossamer wings.
Madness fills her sails.
Tacking them to a shore
Where dreams have come to die.

Expensive

Dreams are supposed to be free
Cheap, at least, had for the taking
But mine exact a price, I see
Dreams like mine are dear to me
As they are nothing like to faking.

The cost taken is slightly akin
To the pound of flesh, in exchange
That Venetian merchant with cruel flint
Found the dreams embedded in my skin
He sought deep with his savage blade.

I give it gladly, the dream I bear
For it's mine, and none can emulate
Nor take, nor raise, nor bring to air
Like flowers plucked without care
In a dusty, lovely wine bottle vase.

Expensive dreams, these ones I hold
And carry, and feed with my existence
They are often brash, and always bold
Untouched by time, never growing old
And strengthened by my persistence.

The price not paid in coin or favor
The laughing merchant seeks his due
In gondolas where the mandolins savor
The sweet and fertile mind's cool flavor
My spirit sings, oft in a bluer hue.

Take your price, oh merchant merry
And keen my soul's sweet tune
The melody will never tarry
The life in the blooms you cannot bury
'Tis worth the debt that I assume.

It's Not Supposed to be This Way

Ambition never happened
And she dreamed her fruitless dreams
In a cluttered room
In a cluttered mind
Filled with wonders and musings
And incomprehensible jumbles
Of dust mice and metaphor.
Skeletons of what should have been
Echoes of shouts,
Better, faster, more.

Clinging to the hope
That something would happen
Misdirected prayers
Misdirected energy
For the deus ex machina
To drop from the sky in his golden chariot
And rescue her from herself.
To make her what she might have been.
What she was told to be.

All the college rock in the world
Won't make her what she isn't
Won't take her back to vicarious ambitions
Donald Fagen sings hollow
In the backdrop of her memory

*But she wasn't there.
Faux intellectualism
With just enough bullshit to pass
For a while, at least.*

*It wasn't supposed to be this way
Living this white-trash life
In this nouveau-riche mind
With all the soul of a 'hood born sistah
The jazz rhythms of a sixties beatnik
No place for the disco baby spinning down
Born time out of mind
Mind out of time,
Brubeck and Byrne make you smarter
But it's the same as it ever was.*

*Fading flower, faded child
Illuminated from within by knowing
Shadows on her face from longing
Never fulfilled
Ever renewed wishes
Irresponsible, they say
What do they know of the machinations
Of the ever so gifted dreamer
And the cold kindling of ambition unlit.*

Don't tell her she should be more
She could be more
It's hard enough to be what she is
And live with the decisions
The turntables turned
To the B-side of life.
She never made the hit parade, you see.
She had a good beat, but was afraid to dance.
It wasn't supposed to be this way.

The song still lives within her
Lilting rhythm of word and phrase
Tilting at the windmill of her life still
Never acquiescing, just depleted.
Running out of juice, you see.
Running out of time to be
The star of the silvered dream.
Number one with a bullet
She holds it fast between her teeth
And bites hard, tasting the metal
And the powder
And the finality of reality.
It wasn't supposed to be this way.

Afloat

Clutching at the sides, smooth worn sides
Finger marks of old grooved into the marble
Cold edges with bitter residue slipping
Between fingers in finger marks marking new grooves
While the ripples grow into waves and crash
And wave murk and mire crushing breath
Out of the soul that grasps and slips and sighs
Drowning again in the dream of escape, release, relent
Once more no relenting once more the dream once more
Feeling the breath leave and the death weave
And the sides heave laughing and passing and gasping
In the exuberant dance of victory, the winning side
Again it wins again it sighs
Again the soul dies.

The Vapor of Dreams

To release my dreams into this vapor
Where they join with fantastical visions,
Above our heads caper
Glorying in each other,
Simple joy in existence, of realization.

This craft I hone daily, yet shroud
From the teeth of the outside world,
Now soars in irrepressible ecstasy
And takes on life outside my regard,
At the touch of fresh air and fraternity.

Yes, there are other fancies
Floating overhead in imagination's liberty,
Rarely encountering others' harmony.
Then meeting, they dance together
In a rambunctious frolic of victory

Dreams released for the world to see
And dismiss or embrace, as they like,
They leap and cavort in outrageous delight
And care not of others theories,
Their delight is simply to have leave.

Creeping Back and Away Again

Here it comes again
The blue fog over my spirit
The pain over my soul
Creeping back, my friend Despair.

It leaves then returns
When I least expect it
I ask what the point is
To continuing this desperate life.

I think of escape
Plan my release, half playfully
But half serious, and afraid.
Despair sits and laughs at me.

Looking for hope, I find none
Looking for reason, there is less
I look back at Despair and ask
"Are you all there is?"

Despair says "yes".

Then a note, a contact
A smile and the beginning of laughter
A concerned question and I know
Despair lied to me again.

There's more than this
There's reason to hope
Life won't be denied so easily
So quickly forsaken.

Despair heads for the door
And looks back with a grin
"I'll be back, you know."
"Yes, and I'll be ready for you then."

"I've come back, and brought hope with me."

Essays

Hawk

I stood in the meadow, and my eye was caught by a hawk circling over the pines. It was a beautiful and elemental creature, full of exuberance in the warm air, rejoicing in the day at hand and all the possibilities therein. It let out a call, high and sweet in the wind, and swept towards the high grass beyond the mown meadow. Searching in the grass were a dozen or so killdeer, their white neckerchiefs gleaming in the sun, calling to each other in their gay voices. Then one sensed the hawk nearby. The alarm went out in a flash and the carefree killdeer sprung off the meadow and dashed into the tall grass, no doubt to protect the young hidden there. The hawk slid across the tips of the grass and back up, making an aeronautic masterpiece. A sudden startled flock of small brown birds leapt out of the grass and in perfect formation like an army dashed off to their nests. The hawk observed this, his red wingtips flashing as he circled. Back into the sky, as a pair of swallows sped across in a panic, purple tails twitching and their ruddy undersides heaving, to save their family from the airborne menace above. Blindly they went, their haste obvious in the chattering talk they were having as they flew. Again the hawk circled. He cast an amused glance at the meadow, then looked my way. I saluted his bright and intelligent eye, respecting his respect for his prey. He seemed to address me with the song of his graceful flight, telling me that he had to keep them alert that the strongest might survive his hunger. Telling me that he enjoyed the game he played with the lesser birds there. Telling me he understood the way of nature and its logic. The beautiful creature went higher and higher into the sky, his bronze feathers gleaming in the late afternoon sun, and then sped back down to the pine trees, calling again to his mate, and telling her of his sport. She rose to join him, and they disappeared into the trees.

Shade

Yesterday my ornamental cherry tree was a lovely sculpture of bare branches; the occasional desiccated fruit hanging tenaciously, left from last year. The sunlight streamed through my window, making the crystal hanging there wink prisms into the living room. The sun was warm, lovely, full of life. I went to work with a smile, thinking of how soon the tulips would begin to bloom, joining the silly daffodils. The daffodils multiplied over the winter, and soon I will have to dig them up. Most of the tulips are recent plantings, though, and I don't even know what color some of them are. They don't need dividing yet. After the tulips, everything starts to happen in the yard. It's already happening, but subtly. Leaves, branches, buds. In a month, the color will be singing. For the moment, it's the hyacinths, the daffodils, snowdrops, and anemones. Mostly purple, and calming, but for the forsythia, which spikes wildly along the fence in the back. I ought to tame it into well-behaved bushes, but I don't have the heart to attempt to constrain it into shape. I looked for the first swelling of the buds on the rhododendrons, but no sign of life yet. It's early.

The birds are returning now. This morning a cardinal sang the most exuberant song I have ever heard from a wire. He was advertising, I think. The brilliant red head was thrown back and from the swollen throat came a song of the sweetest, most confident notes. I haven't seen any robins yet, though I've heard them. Sometimes I sit on the porch and watch the robins, their heads cocked sideways, listening for the rustle of worms underground. They watch, hop, and listen. Then a sudden jab of the beak into the ground. It's amazing that they can actually hear the worms. If my hearing were that acute, I'd go mad.

When I came home from work yesterday, I looked up into the tree for the little finch nest in the crook of a branch. They've been living there for a couple of years now, ever since our little feral cat moved on.

It's safe for them now. I couldn't see the nest. The tree was covered with leaves. Small, red tinged leaves, but enough to provide shade where there was no shade before. Right on time, as usual. I couldn't help but look for the buds that will make the tree explode into pink decadence. They were there, but tiny. If I'm remembering correctly, in a week or so they will start to open, then a week or so after that, the fragrance will be incredible. As soon as the scent reaches its peak, the flowers will leave a carpet of pink petals on the steps, the grass, the walkway. I like the way it looks, so I don't sweep them up. It causes a mess later, but it's worth it to have that pink carpet. Once the blossoms are done, the leaves grow very fast, shade just when you need it. As the sun coming in through the window becomes unbearably warm, it is mercifully filtered by the leaves. Their shadows move enough to allow the occasional sunbeam to strike the crystal.

I don't mind the trade. The flowers are prettier, anyway.

Millooneyum Halftime

This year, I had the dubious pleasure of observing the strangest halftime show I've ever seen. I've seen a few in my lifetime, being a diehard football fan, one of those rare birds who actually wants to watch the game for the game.

While the Super Bowl is usually a place where one expects to see at least one good team, the halftime show has long been the refuge of musical mediocrity. The dawn of the new millennium saw no change in that sad standard.

We were treated to a chorus of what appeared to be well over 100 "flying nuns" with Tweedle-dum and Tweedle-dee style habits. The top part of their white robes was distended at the hip-line by a hula-hoop sort of contraption, which jiggled back and forth disconcertingly as they moved their arms. They seemed to be having some kind of spastic reaction to Christina Aguilera and Enrique Iglesias singing together. Who could blame them? While this less-than-sublime aural experience was going on, an inflatable goddess or god of dubious ethnicity and gender identity was puffed up over the stadium. Then came the beloved giant stick figures. Dancing amidst these emaciated Michelin men were black clad people with balloon animals attached at all angles to their heads. Rainbow color poodles. Or dachshunds. Or giraffes. I don't know what demented clown constructed these headgear augmentations, but he needs therapy. Edward James Olmos waxed philosophic about unity and tolerance and the millennium, or something. I don't know why he was there. If his purpose was to make sense, it didn't work. Maybe he was trying to explain the marching band that had furry snail shells on their heads.

Then came Phil Collins. He tried, he really did. It was hard to listen to him, though, because I was distracted trying to figure out why he had a neon green amusement park armband on his wrist. He was lifted about halfway up the inflatable deity on a platform made of broken mirrors. I don't know what he was singing. At one point during his song, the cameras panned back to reveal the percussion section of the band wearing "Hellraiser" hats. You know, with the silver knitting needles poking out in every direction.

I continued watching in grim fascination. It was like watching a car accident. Stranger things kept appearing. The lovely Toni Braxton was surrounded by a host of 20-foot stick figure dragonflies, no doubt putting her in fear for her safety, not to mention her hairstyle. Mr. Olmos made another ghostly appearance to say…something else. I couldn't hear him through the incredible visual distractions. Then, the balloon deity began deflating and its robes opened so that a live person wearing the same costume could emerge. Still couldn't place ethnicity or gender on this poor soul. Too much gold paint. Throughout, the chorus of flying Tweedle-dums and Tweedle-dees kept twitching. I sympathized with them. I felt like Hunter S. Thompson in "Fear and Loathing in Las Vegas" but without the dangerous drugs.

I have yet to figure out what it all meant, but I think it had something to do with either world peace and unity, or going to Disney world to see more of the same. But if this is what Disney's like these days, leave your kids home. It could scar them irreparably.

Pondering Y2K

December 31, 1999.

I wonder if anything will be different tomorrow, other than having a strange and cumbersome date to place, carefully and with aforethought every time, on our checks and letters.

I never believed that the world was ending, or even that an apocalypse of convenience was about to occur. Up until yesterday, I planned to be on the Internet at 12:01 am, 1/1/2000. I may still be there, but in a break with convention, I've actually been invited to two different gatherings. Strange that this should happen this year, when so much has changed in the last day. My personal world has changed in great ways, with the loss of a friend and the strain in family relationships, but this has occurred before the dawn of the New Year. In the sunset of 1999, ominous things gathered at my door and manifested their dark presence while the world prepared to party.

I watch people at work, walking through the halls and going about their day as usual. Most of them seem to have an air of expectation. Not so much worry as simple anticipation, wondering what will happen, wondering the same things that I wonder. They carry the same papers and folders and briefcases and coffee mugs as any other day. Will they be disappointed if nothing cataclysmic occurs tomorrow? The computer programmers and fixers and equipment services people will be here all weekend. I envy them their party, in some ways. To be in these halls after dark, with no corporate bigwigs present, with pizza and pop and no doubt, smuggled champagne and beer, just watching and waiting. Will they dance to music that plays from their CD ROM drives? Maybe. At 12:01, will the music stop? I doubt it.

People are driving around with the same strange expressions on their faces. They peer through car windows at the sunlight and observe. Are they observing as keenly as I am? Do they wonder what the morrow will bring? At the post office, the postmaster makes his last pickup at the outside boxes at noon. Having placed two final items into the box, I watched him open the blue door and remove the mail. His key winked self important in the sun. He closed the door and patted the envelopes in the bin, with what might have been an air of finality, but was more likely my own hypersensitive state of observation. Who is to say there's any finality about this day? The only sure finality is that we are no longer going to be starting the year section of dates with the number one.

Maybe people are anticipating something more. I am almost certain they are. Great omens and portents accompany this New Year, not the least of which was the largest full moon in 137 years. The longest night, lit by the brightest light. A sign of hope? Or a forecast for disaster? As always, it's all in how you see it. There are those that see this as the dawning of a great new age, a new enlightenment in learning and human understanding and faith. There are those who will accept nothing less than disaster, death, the second or third coming of the end of the world, the foretold "end times" that are ever predicted but never transpiring. What shall we do about these self-proclaimed prophets of the apocalypse? My suggestion is to allow natural selection to run its course, and hope they don't take too many innocent souls along for the ride. Like the meteorologists that drool and chomp at the bit with every tropical wave, hoping for the hurricane that will end all hurricanes, they will be sorely disappointed and perhaps will engineer their own end, so that they will be right. Dead, but right.

My dog greets me at the door with his usual elated smile. He doesn't know what day it is. He doesn't care. I shouldn't either, and in truth, I don't. As an observer of human behavior, however, it is a once in a lifetime opportunity to watch reactions and marvel at the range of character found in our species. To feel the collective indrawn breath as the second hand nears midnight, the rush of fear and celebration, and then what? Then what? I do not know. The observation will continue tomorrow, and I will search the faces, watch the footsteps, find smiles and relief and disgust and hangovers. Most likely, no different from any other year. Perhaps a bit more relief.

    The people in my office talk seriously about the impending change. They wonder about bombs and nuclear power plants and electrical systems. We speculate about what's coming. The conclusion is made if anything disastrous were to happen, it would have happened already. It's already past midnight in half the world. What do their faces look like, in the Philippines, in New Zealand? Are the New Delhians dancing in the streets, or cowering under their beds? Is all well out there? Will Hawaii be watching for our reaction? And how do they feel, being last? To ride nearly astride the date line, as Umberto Eco called it, "The Island of the Day Before". On the other side of the line, it's a New Year. When the midnight moon crosses that line, we will all be into the future. We can wave a fond goodbye to the year, the decade, the century. We can put aside "no year zero" debates about the veracity of the record keeping. We can contrast our calendar with the calendar of other cultures and see that it is good, or at least that it works for us. Millennia have gone by for, well, millennia. Entering the true new millennium one year from today will not have the same impact. It's all about the number 2, and the fact that almost everyone in the world will spend the better part of a month thinking very carefully before they write the date in their checkbooks. And it's all about reflecting on where we've come in two thousand years, the current era standing beneath our feet and the new beginning stretching out above and around us. It's a wonderful chance for humanity to become more human, to become more enlightened, to gain newfound respect for life and earth and sky and water. For each other. For ourselves.

Denver

I am not from Denver. I have never even been there, except twice at the airport on a stopover. It's a beautiful place, from what I could see. I don't think Denver is the problem.

Two children, social rejects, from what we are given to understand, killed fifteen people. They did it with weapons they should never have had. They did it with high explosives, grenades, bombs. The potential for even more death was there; thankfully, it was limited to fifteen.

My first reaction was "not again". Then it was "where are their parents?" Then it was "where did they manage to obtain such an arsenal?" No answers. The press salivates over this occurrence, as they always have and always will. Big news, kids go on a rampage at their high school. Kids clad in black trench coats, they were pariahs, desperados. Getting even. Getting even with other kids, with teachers, with society. Guess they showed us. What did they show us?

They showed us how sad it is to be alone. How sad it is to be a child in today's society, a child with few friends, with anger, with unresolved pain.

How lonely and afraid they must have been when they fired the first shots. How did they feel when they realized people were really dying, that it wasn't a game? Were they relieved when their own death came?

I wonder how their parents feel. When my father killed himself, his father spent the rest of his life retracing his footsteps, to see what he might have done differently. He eventually was lost there, and died with very little memory of anything. I can imagine the parents of these boys, their grief, their despair, wishing they could go back and change things. Even when parents are not necessarily responsible, they take responsibility. It's just how we are. All parents should use this as an opportunity to change things now, before it's too late. Before this happens again.

But the sad fact is, they won't. The news will move from lead story to second page to human-interest articles or stories of survival in the magazine section of the Sunday paper, and then it will be forgotten. We all rubberneck at the scene of an accident, but we don't slow down on the curve next time. We bury our heads in the sand, and rest assured it won't happen to us. Our town is different; it's not Denver, or Oklahoma City. Our town is not Kosovo. People just don't do things like that here. So, we go on with our lives, our work, our habits of not really listening to our kids, not really noticing what they're doing. We don't see that we all live in Denver.

Choose to remember what you will from this tragedy. Remember the gory pictures, remember the fear of the parents. Remember the grim faces of the police. Remember the sense of isolation the killers felt when they planned this massacre. Remember that it could have been worse.

Most of all, remember that it could have been your child.

Greta and Max

They play so well together. I marvel at the easy relationship between these two. Greta is my mother's Weimaraner, a huge grey ghostly dog with human eyes and a sedate nature. She was rescued from a shelter, having been abused and neglected her whole life, then tagged for euthanasia. A Weimaraner owner picked her up and my mother got her from him, the beginning of a unique and friendly relationship.

Max is my dog. He's a Pembroke Welsh Corgi, a little steam engine of a dog, deep brown typical puppy dog eyes, fiercely protective and playful. He considers his herd his domain, and any intruders are regarded suspiciously for days, weeks sometimes. He hasn't known a day of want or neglect in his whole life, and as a dog will do, he knows which side his bread is buttered on.

I watch them interact, Max initiating play, Greta too tired and hot to follow. She feels bad though, and licks Max's muzzle. He joyfully kisses her back, and allows her to lie down. He lays a short distance from her; head on paws, and regards her with his liquid eyes with fascination and adoration. Greta looks at him with half-lidded eyes and a smile on her face; they have the ideal relationship. Max rolls over on his back and Greta nuzzles his chest affectionately. No pressure there, no expectations. They simply love and enjoy each other.

Greta and Max are filled with joy and rediscovery at every new meeting. Familiar companions, joyously sniffing each other, recalling past play times, never regretting the time they are apart, simply loving the opportunity to spend more time together. They circle each other, Max short enough to walk under Greta's legs, Greta bowing her head to meet his. Greta pounces forward catlike, front paws outstretched on the ground to get Max to play. He runs to her and tugs at her ear carefully, prompting her to roll onto the ground in front of him. She leaps up and pounces at him again, and he takes off at a full run around the house like a tiny locomotive. She barks at him, not menacingly but teasing, and places herself in his path forcing him to either weave or stop. Sometimes he simply drops onto the floor in front of her and exposes his tummy, conceding to her size and strength. Sometimes she rolls over in front of him, in respect for his friendship and trust for his kindness.

I have seen Max and Greta play together countless times. Greta is older and so more sedate, but if she is in the right mood it is quite a romp. She seldom initiates play, but when she does, the delight in Max is tangible. Greta is twice his size easily, but she treats Max as an equal, and he appreciates it. They roll on the floor together, Greta nipping at Max's furry chest in a grooming fashion. Max's head back and tongue lolling out in delight, then back up for another few dozen laps around the dining room table.

I wonder often why people can't get along more like Greta and Max do. Tolerant, understanding, loving. Is it a function of their lower brain capacity that they argue less and love more? Or is it that our brains are too complex to simply enjoy each other without demand or suspicion? I watch the dogs together and try to emulate their generosity of spirit. The joy in their eyes as they play and the contentment as they rest is so very desirable.

Greta looks at me with her ghostly eyes and her innocent smile, face drawn up in such a perfect imitation of a human smile, like a child. She shows her age and her character in her eyes, but her bad past experiences are nowhere to be found. She trusts me entirely and loves with all her canine heart. I respect her trust and wouldn't dream of betraying it. Her stub of tail wiggles enthusiastically whenever she sees me, putting her paws on my shoulders to give me kisses in greeting. I pat her head and call her "my sister Greta," looking in her grey eyes with appreciation for her love.

Max is my child. No less than that. He has a place in my heart second only to my children, and he earns it daily. He shows utter devotion in his eyes, his happiness at my return and his indignance at my departures.

Fiercely protective, his herding nature keeps us in his constant watch, but he is never overbearing. He lays in my arms like a baby sometimes, all 30 pounds of stocky little dog, looking up at me with adoration. It's so fulfilling to have a living being regard you that way.

Max and Greta have different natures, but their natures mesh with each other perfectly. They trust, they play, and they tolerate. When the time comes, they go separately without tears and simply appreciate the time together. This is truly something we can aspire to. To not want knowledge of the future, to not worry about what tomorrow brings, but just to rejoice in the time we have together.

Greta and Max teach us all a valuable lesson if we watch and pay attention to their interaction. Tolerate, love, and give space where needed. That's the best possible definition of "a dog's life."

1420 Franklin Avenue

The house itself is caught between the urban and the suburban, not quite far out enough to qualify as the 'burbs but not close enough to be in the city. Dark brown brick, the porch triple arches that in the summer were gaily topped with red and yellow striped awnings. I can still see my Grandfather up on the ladder, gamely doing battle with the unruly canvas, his bald head sweating as he mumbled curses in the sour twang of his Texan birth. My Grandmother would come out occasionally to mark his progress and perhaps to comment on the quality of his work, or the lack thereof. It seems to me in the dim light of memory that she occasionally brought him a beer as he labored. More often than not though, she was busy with her beauty shop, or with cooking something, or cleaning, she was never at rest that I can recall.

My Grandmother was a short woman, darkly and beautifully Italian, in that wonderful Italian matron way that is so impossible to achieve unless you're born to it. Thick black hair, gracefully streaked with gray and silver, she exuded power, control, and love in equal measure. She had immense dark brown eyes, intelligent and intense, the same eyes that I see when I look into my elder daughter's face. The "Fusco" eyes that have gone on in 4 generations of my family, undiluted and identical, beautiful and full of life and operatic melodrama. Her skin was olive, smooth but for the occasional beauty mark, her mouth full and set in a determined fashion, her nose large and slightly hooked, my mothers nose, and a more pronounced version of my own. Her hands were always carefully manicured, but years of hard work were evident on the fingers and palms. She wore an amethyst and silver ring on her right hand and her wedding band on the left. The amethyst fascinated me, the way it would sparkle and sometimes change color in the light and according to her mood. She knew my affection for it and promised it would be mine someday. I wear it now every day as I watch my knuckles thicken and my carefully manicured hands begin to resemble hers. Her knuckles showed that slight thickening that means arthritis in years to come, and the stain of permanent wave solution and hair dye were on her palms. Her arms were powerful and had the middle aged droop of the upper arm, the slight waving of lax muscles that carried babies for years and now only carried the weight of her endless cooking, her endless work, her endless worry for her family and the bitterness of her marriage. She had a half-dollar sized scar on her upper arm from a smallpox vaccine gone bad, I asked her about it many times in that fascination that children have with the irregularities of their elders. Sitting in the kitchen, the copper Jell-O molds hanging decoratively from the walls, the brown cabinets with their coppery handles and the smells of the last sauce, the last cake, the last batch of cookies in the air. The ghastly yellow wallpaper behind the kitchen table, the vintage 50's Formica topped table and padded vinyl chairs that were so comfortable except in the summer when your legs stuck to them in the heat. I sat watching my grandmother cook a pot of Farina for my breakfast. She stood over the stove, legs apart, solid black shoes, stockings and a print dress, a working class Donna Reed, sans pearls. She held total control over all kitchen functions, or God help the hapless appliances that stood in her way.

"Gram, what happened to your arm?"

She removed the Pall Mall from her mouth, took another sip of coffee and told me.

"It was a vaccination, baby." She always called me "baby"; I was her first and only grandchild and the love of her life.

"Why did it get so big, Gram?"

"Because I had a bad reaction to the shot. It got infected, and now I have a big scar there."

Her voice was deep and resonant, another familial trait, reaching through all branches of the family, through me and into my children.

"Did it hurt?" I was amazed that anything was capable of hurting my grandmother.

"Of course it hurt." She stirred the cereal for the final time and emptied the contents of the pot into a soup bowl for me. As she placed the bowl in front of me, I looked again at the scar, respecting its power over my gram and at the same time despising it for hurting her, the woman that I loved above all else. She looked down at me as she spooned margarine and sugar into the hot cereal. "It wasn't that bad, now eat your breakfast so you can go to school." I added a bit of milk and stirred the contents of the bowl into a delicious gruel, as the morning sky began to lighten. As I ate, I watched her move around the kitchen, dishcloth over her shoulder; her hands full of last night's clean dishes as she emptied the dishwasher and began her day. There were lumps in the Farina. There were always small lumps, nothing big and choking, just enough to give it added texture and interest, to my mind. One morning, my mother made it for me. She stirred and stirred, careful to add the white granules slowly so it would be perfect. She presented me with the bowl, the proper proportions of margarine and sugar and milk, I stirred and tasted and asked, "Where are the lumps? I wanted lumps!" My poor mother was dismayed. Now, I can imagine how she must have felt, a hopelessly young woman trying to assert her motherhood in a home that already had an absolute mother, an absolute queen. She only wanted to please me, and I only wanted my grandmother's lumps in my cereal.

The kitchen was the center of activity, but the dining room was the center of the family. Dinner was eaten there, a grand presentation of my Grandmother's culinary mastery. The dining room had a large window overlooking the back yard, and my Grandfather sat at the head of the table, his head and shoulders framed in the window. On his left, a glass front buffet cabinet with the good china, the good glassware, and the eternal bottle of Old Grand Dad in its rocking dispenser on top. On his right, the enclosed china cabinet with the less-fancy china and my Grandmother's collection of teacups. A buffet sat along the wall and everything gleamed clean and shining. Pap was a Texan by birth, and he never really adjusted to living in the north. He was thin, wiry strong and seemed so tall, but only stood about 5 ft 6. I was taller than he by the time I was 16 years old. Bald, with large eyeglasses standing out on his face, his hands with their long fingers always holding a piece of bread at the dinner table, that's how I see him now. He had a set of enormous white dentures that had a permanent residence in the bathroom cabinet, on the top shelf, in a medium sized tumbler. I would look at them amazed as a child and wonder what they'd look like in his mouth, if it would change him, or make him smile more. He was sour, unsmiling, underemployed. A man perplexed by the end result of his life, seeming to wait for something to happen to wake him up and take him back to the arid plains of Texas to start over again. He had a rather nasal voice, a decided accent, though his speech was free from southern expressions. I don't believe that my Grandmother would have permitted them in her home. He was somewhat mechanically inclined, and I spent many a fascinated hour pondering the mysteries of his shop area in the basement. The tools so exotic and strange, but he knew the form and function of every one. He could fix anything; build just about anything, but there was no joy or pride in it for him. I think the combined effects of alcohol and my Grandmother were too much for him. He plugged along in his life and I suppose made the most of it in his own way. There was a great deal of anger buried in him and very little humor. The living room was his domain; he stayed in the chair in front of the TV, his feet up on the vinyl ottoman, a cold Iron City Beer on the end table next to him. When I was young, we had a large color console television, it stood across from Pap's chair, and at right angles to the built in bookshelves that held the encyclopedias. There were glass block windows above the bookshelves, one on either side of the mantelpiece. I loved the murky views to be seen there, much more interesting to wonder what was to be seen rather than looking at the side of the neighbor's house. Eventually, the television developed a similar murkiness. Pap was not good with electronics, but he wasn't prepared to admit defeat, so he kept the console and placed a large portable color television on top of it. It stayed that way for years, the console was never moved to the workshop in the basement, but it was never disposed of either. When the second television bled its life away many years later, Pap got a small black and white portable that had been in one of the bedrooms. He placed it on top of the second television, making a pyramid, or was it a cairn, of televisions there, two blank and dead and the third dim with age. It was a monument to his ambivalence. He never seemed to find it odd, but it fascinated me and irritated my mother and her siblings. My Grandmother didn't appear to care about the pyramid, as long as it kept my Pap happy and out of her way.

Pap didn't show much emotion, other than occasionally anger or frustration. But there was love there. What little humor he had was in an odd sense, like giving Indian burns and noogies. I fell for it countless times.

"Hey, did I ever show you how the cow ate the cabbage?"
"No, Pap, you didn't."

He had, many times. For some reason, I never remembered.

"Like this!"
"OUCH!"

A painful crunching of fingers jawlike into the skin above my knee, and I remembered how the cow ate the cabbage. Poor cabbage. It wasn't all bad, though. When I was seven years old, I had my tonsils out. Gram was working every day after I returned from the hospital, and my mother was in school. I spent the days with Pap. I remember sitting on the living room floor playing Crazy Eights or maybe it was Go Fish on the hassock with Pap, and him getting me popsicles to ease the ache in my throat. He was gruff, but I suppose he loved as much as he was able. I think he felt that he'd be betraying his discontent by showing any sign of happiness at life, any sign of enjoyment in his children or grand child. He showed me more of affection than he showed anyone else. There is a letter saved in a family photo album, from my Aunt Non to my Grandfather, sent to him when he was away in WWII, on the occasion of my Mother's birth. This letter is very telling as to his character, as are the ones that followed in replies. Non writes that he is the father of a beautiful baby girl named Arlene Jo. She hopes that he isn't too disappointed that it isn't the boy he had hoped for, but conveys certainty that the next one will be. She proceeds to sell him on his daughter, speaks of her beauty, of her health, and points out to him that she is his namesake even though a girl. (His name was Arlie) Perhaps they were afraid that he wouldn't return from the war. My Gram addressed the letter as if it were the baby talking.

Hello Pop—I just arrived at 745. I'm a little girl and I weigh exactly 7 pounds and 4 ounces. I hope you love me as much as Mom and me love you.

Guess you would like to know the color of my eyes and hair. My eyes are black and my hair is black too.

This was obviously written before the birth, the pertinent facts are written into underlined areas, as if filled in later. Non continues the letter.

This is Nell and I sure hope that you wont be disappointed by the package that just arrived this evening for the stork delivered a girl instead of a boy and all Fran keeps saying is tell Arlie I couldn't help it, honest. So perhaps you'll understand how she feels. By the way, it was a stubborn little tyke, we had a hard time delivering that package but rest at ease for the mother and baby are doing nicely especially the baby she is trying to chew her hands already. A chip off the old block.

Fran said she would call the baby Arlene Jo and hopes you'll like it. We are all rejoicing about the girl so I hope you can rejoice with us and perhaps the boy will follow later on.

I read the letter you wrote on the 20th to Fran and when I read "all my love to you and our boy," she cried like the devil because it wasn't. Gosh, I wish it were a boy now too.

Well Arlie, I hope you are well and maybe you can write her a letter and make her understand that it is all right.

We all extend our congratulations for you and hope you'll be home soon to enjoy the baby and life as a whole.

All our love to you and Fran sends all her love to you also.

As Ever

Your Sis
Nell.

He wrote letters back, heavily army-censored. Lovely letters addressed to his daughter, reassuring her of his love and telling her that they would meet soon. I wonder what happened to change this affectionate man into the distant icon that he was by the time I happened along.

Feb 4th 1945
Germany
My Dear Little Miss Pin-Up

It's about time for me to write you a letter. Of course, you can let your Mother read this if you want, it's up to you. I want to tell you that you are the Pin Up of this platoon and the company if I have much to do with it. Say I can hardly wait for that picture of you when you were a baby. Frances said she took a picture of you when she brought you home. If you ask me you had better get her on the ball and send them on. Say I haven't heard from her in about 3 days. I think it would be very nice of you if you could find time to write. That is if you ain't too busy going out. Take good care when you go out to the night clubs. One of the boys was asking me if you went to the USO's to help keep the boys happy. I told him I hoped not because all the guys are wolfs and I know it. Say I hear you go in for sports. What do you play? I can bet you are the best at any game.

Honey tell that Mother of yours to get on the ball and write me and be sure to send pictures of you as often as she can.

Please give my regards to your Grand-Mother and Grand-Pop and to all your aunts and uncles. Well do give all my love to your mother.

Your Pop

Not many of these letters survive, but they are remarkable in their tone and the insecurity, the humanity, of the man that wrote them. He was a lonely soldier that missed his family, badly. He was a husband and father that loved his wife and daughter.

Feb 14th 1945
Germany

My Darling Little Pin Up-

I wrote that mother of yours but just in case she don't read it to you, the best thing for me to do is write straight to you. She is pretty good to write, I can say that for her. I guess she is still as sweet as she was when I left but she may just be the least conceited now that she has you to herself. Honey if I was home with her the two of us would show you off to all the neighbors and friends. There is some chance that your mother is the same sweet person. I would for sure like to be there to be sure she loves me yet. She writes me every day and tells me of her love and I don't doubt it but would like to be there. Honey, please give all the folks my love and regards on sweet Valentines Day. Love to you and your Mother

Just Dad

A very different man than the one I knew. All my life I will wonder what changed him so, and I will never learn for sure. He showed nothing more than glimpses of that loving man in the seventeen years that I knew him.

The basement of the house was a wonderful place for a child. Beginning with the stairs and the shelves at the top, filled with cleaning supplies, everyday tools and things that just didn't go anywhere else, down to the small landing where my Gram's beauty shop clients would enter, down to the shop itself. The smell of shampoo and rinse and the magic she performed on her customers rose up the stairs and called me down. The first room at the bottom of the steps was the wash and set area, and the shampoo sink with its reclining chair was the first thing you saw. I can still feel Gram's fingers scrubbing my head briskly when she would wash my hair there. She was very enthusiastic about washing; my scalp still tingles at the memory of her attention. There was a large mirror on the wall in the center of the room with the chair for setting hair in front of it, then 2 chairs for waiting clients on the far wall, a small table that held magazines and a bottle of combs in Barbasol between them. In the back room of the salon were the dryers, three of them, their mechanical heads poised at the ready for the next customer, and a manicure table on wheels so she could do their nails as they dried. The whole shop was paneled in a pleasing caramel brown, and the floor was pink linoleum. If you went around to the right at the foot of the stairs, there was a step down into the rest of the basement. My Grandfather's workshop was there, behind the beauty shop, a room with a cantankerous door that let out a squeal whenever one tried to open it. It seemed it was always dim inside that room, lit only by a bulb above the workbench that was turned on and off by screwing and unscrewing it. There was a refrigerator that held a case of beer and a case of Regent Soda at all times, and beside it, the empty cases waiting to be filled with the spent bottles and returned to the distributors. My Grandmother had a desk in the middle of the larger basement area that held her accounting supplies for the household and her shop. Under the stairs and behind this desk, was a storage area where the Christmas decorations lived, boxes upon boxes waiting for the next holiday to be set up and enjoyed again. There was a set of trains that my Grandfather put up under the tree, and the boxes of blue and multicolored lights that went around the triple arches of the porch. The joy of watching these boxes being taken out and opened every year was indescribable. That was the first gift of the holidays.

Opposite the desk was a room that my Uncle Ray and Uncle George built as a sort of rumpus room. They were 13 and 14 years older than I was respectively and so were more like siblings than uncles. We grew up together, my uncles and my Aunt Renee and my Mother and I. I wanted so much to be a part of their world, of their generation, and in many ways, I was, but there were barriers, and the room there was one of these. I was welcomed there of course, but was never comfortable with their friends, like a pesky kid sister. The room had cast off furniture of a horrifying green color, that color that was never seen again after 1970 and rightfully so. An old coffee table sat amid the couch and the loveseat and the chair. They had gone to a carpet store and acquired the leavings of past installations to cover the floor. These were not remnants but rather scraps of carpet, and my uncles and my Mother patiently pieced them together in a jigsaw. It was a wonderful floor, the different textures and colors of carpet joyful to the eye and to the feet. Many years later, when I lived in that house after my Grandfather's death, I used that room as a darkroom. Standing in front of the table that held my equipment in the dark, the ghostly light from the enlarger lighting my work and nothing else, I could feel that carpet under my feet, and see the patchwork. I can still feel it, the contrasting fabrics under bare feet. Leaving that room and its mingled smells of tobacco and incense and fresh wood, to the left and through a doorway was the laundry room. And in the laundry room was one of the most fascinating objects in the whole house, the mangle.

It sat there, opposite the washer and dryer, an ancient peeling kitchen chair in front of it, so alien, so intimidating, a mechanical mystery. I watched it from the corner of my eye for most of my childhood, anticipating the moment when that gaping mouth would either speak or attempt to gobble me up. My Grandmother sat in front of it, a basket of damp sheets at her feet, and fed them into the mangle one at a time. It devoured them and spat them out dry, pressed and fragrant. This was before the invention of fitted sheets; I often wonder what the mangle would have made of them. As with any other appliance, Gram's mastery over the mangle was complete. The damp mess at her feet was transformed into a neat crisp bundle ready to go into the linen closet. My Mother and my Aunt Renee both had singed their fingers countless times, and I never worked up nerve enough to attempt to use it. Some things were better left alone.

Up the stairs to the linen closet, I sometimes helped my Grandmother put the things away, but more often than not, she did it herself. The closet was set into a recess in front of the bathroom, gleaming varnished oak doors with brass latches. There were stacks and stacks of towels, sheets, dishcloths, blankets and quilts. It was the largest linen closet I have ever seen. The upstairs of the house wasn't particularly large; it had 3 bedrooms and a bath. The largest bedroom was my Grandparents' and was in the front of the house. My mother and I stayed in the room on the side; it overlooked the back yard and the dark brick of the neighbors' house. The third bedroom belonged to my Aunt Renee, 9 years my senior. I can't for the life of me recall where my uncles slept while they still lived there. I think they were both in the service most of the time I was growing up, and then they moved on and married. The doorknobs of the bedrooms were fascinating. They were cut glass, gleaming like crystal. As a child, I imagined they were diamonds. The door to the master bedroom was propped open with a cast-iron elephant. In the mornings, my Grandfather would stumble out of their room and head for the white-tiled bathroom. After a little while, he would open the door and I would watch in amazement as he shaved with a double-edged razor, making the leavings of soap in his shaving cup foam with a white handled brush. This was an eternal male mystery, how they shaved the hair off their faces, only to have it return in the morning. My Grandfather tolerated my curiosity. I suppose he was somewhat indulgent toward me in his own way. He would cough and spit into the commode (it was never called a toilet), shave, then cough and spit again and flush. We returned to our respective rooms and got dressed for the day, and then I took my clothes and tossed them down the laundry chute. I always watched them fall, my head in the chute, waiting for the soft "fwoosh" of impact at the bottom. That was another marvel of the house to me. I frequently imagined what it would be like to slide down that chute, landing in the soiled clothes at the bottom, or preferably in the basement if the door was open and the work was in progress. Sometimes I feared that Renee would come along and shove me down the chute, laughing as I tumbled to my demise. She had almost as much anger in her as my Grandfather did. Rather than a general undirected anger, her wrath had a target, namely me.

    Renee was a beautiful girl with long braids, a trim figure, and an endless stream of boy and girl friends. She had a huge collection of stuffed animals and Nancy Drew mysteries. She was my hero. Strangely enough, her undisguised contempt for me made me want her love and acceptance more. She resented my displacing her as the baby of the family, resented my cheerful disposition and intelligence, and resented the love and attention that her mother lavished on me. Renee was an extremely bright girl, witty and funny. In my presence, her wit and humor turned to vicious sarcasm. The things she said to me ranged from the simply smart aleck to the downright mean. She was never physically violent; she didn't need to be. Her tongue was weapon enough.

"Oh it's the brat. Eating again?"

"Hi Renee. Are you going to have breakfast?"

"No, I'm not going to have breakfast. I'm just walking around with a box of cereal and a bowl cause I feel like it."

"Very funny."

"You know, if you had a brain you'd be dangerous."

"Would you hand me the milk?"

"What's the matter, are you crippled? Get it yourself."

She was a Girl Scout with a large collection of merit badges and different uniforms; I admired them and asked endless questions about what this or that one meant. I gazed longingly at her books and manuals and aspired toward scout hood myself someday. Somewhere along the line, I realized her contempt and stopped admiring her quite so much, though in many ways, I still do admire her, and we have reached a comfortable truce in our relationship. We have grown older and raised our children, borne our pain and matured. We live in different houses now, but carry 1420 Franklin Avenue with us still.

Ray and George were my uncles. I never referred to them as "Uncle", I was never told to. I suppose I was never encouraged to show them respect out of hand, though they did earn my respect. Ray was the elder brother, second in line to my mother, as intelligent and witty as the rest of the family. He had the "Fusco" eyes and facial features, and my Grandfather's quickly receding hairline. He was terribly angry, though he concealed it well. Dark haired and olive skinned, handsome and funny; he was a wonderful uncle/big brother to me. When I was eight years old, I fell from a wall over an alleyway down the street. My mother rushed to my rescue, having been alerted to the accident by a neighbor child. She realized my leg was broken right away, and carried me to the street. Ray was driving past in his car; an amazing bronze colored Buick Riviera with green tinted windows and a functioning record player under the dash. My mother got us into the front seat of the car and off to the hospital we sped. I suppose this identified Ray to me as the knight in shining armor. I can still see the late afternoon sun coming in through the greenish tint of the front window, and hear my pleas to Ray to drive slower and not hit so many potholes. They both had wonderful cars, that Riviera, George's Mustang, a gleaming streamlined car of metallic green. George took after my Grandfather in looks, he was fairer skinned, and he and Renee looked very alike. George was so talented musically that he could play any instrument you handed him. He had the same sarcastic wit as the rest of his siblings, and an absolutely wonderful sense of humor. I learned that George developed his humor as a defense. My Grandfather had been abusive to his wife, and to his 2 eldest children, my Mother and Ray. He was alcoholic and angry. George made him laugh. Somehow, he managed to hone that humor to a fine enough point to reach his father. I knew none of this, it took adulthood and death and maturity to learn the facts of what lay behind the idyllic veil of my youth. My Mother related a story, Pap was drunk, and in his stupor, asked George "Who are you?" George replied "My name's Cliff, why don't you drop over sometime?" My Grandfather laughed, and some safety was achieved. George built this wall of humor between himself and his father brick by brick, until he was safe.

In the back yard of the house at 1420 Franklin Avenue, there was only one constant and that was the rosebushes. My Grandmother had a love for roses but not enough time to tend the garden the way it deserved, so she kept it to a minimum. As a child, the back yard seemed enormous and the rose bushes were large and constantly flowering. What a shock to return as an adult to see things in their proper scale. It wasn't large; in fact, it was rather small. The yard was always neat and well groomed. For a time, we had a small swimming pool in the yard, nothing elaborate but enough to require a layer of sand as a base. My Grandfather had an enormous metal roller to flatten and even the sand. After the broken leg incident, I was sitting on the doors to the cellar steps one afternoon watching my uncles play whiffle ball. The pool was either gone or inaccessible because of the cast on my leg. I remember how hot and miserable it was as I leaned against the metal roller and wondered what was inside. I moved the handle back and forth, back and forth, and pondered the mystery while the boys played. In an instant, one of my uncles had tripped over my extended leg and cracked the cast. I can't remember if there was pain, all I remember is the dismayed expression on their faces. I don't even remember which one did it. So back to the hospital for another set of X-rays, this time in George's Mustang. To this day, I associate those large metal lawn rollers with the dreadful heaviness the reinforced cast placed upon me. Although there was no further damage to my leg, the incident left me forever suspicious of metal lawn rollers.

Later that same miserable summer, Renee decided that I needed to have my ears pierced. In the naiveté of my adoration for her, I never imagined that she could hurt me. She sat me on the dining room table and brought in rubbing alcohol, a needle and thread, and cotton balls. At least she was quick about it. Before I knew what happened, I had loops of thread hanging from my ears. She patted the new holes down with the alcohol and told me grimly to keep my fingers away from the holes or they would become infected. Remembering my Grandmother's scar, an infection in my earlobes was the last thing I wanted. My mother was horrified when she discovered what Renee had done. But I was delighted to be grown up enough to have earrings. The holes are still crooked, leaning from front to back on one side and from back to front on the other, a permanent reminder of that summer day.

A row of garages stood across the alleyway, in a state of decay that worsened every year. There was the warning issued every time I went out to play; "Stay away from the garages!" In addition to the garages was a large hillside, thick with trees and bushes. This was my playground. I never tired of finding new paths through the trees, new short cuts and long cuts both to Rifugiato's store at the bottom of the hill. The summers brought long treks through these woods, miniature camping expeditions with a thermos of milk and a sandwich. Fall was romping through endless piles of leaves and eating crab apples, and occasionally getting sick from them, but not often. I knew better than to eat too many. Winter was the wonder of sledding down the long hills on different paths, sometimes with an uncle, sometimes with a friend, but most often alone. I was usually alone, not being a popular child, very solitary and introspective. I longed to be one of the popular crowd, but I didn't know how. So endless books, walks, and flights of imagination were my companions through the days of Franklin Avenue. I wasn't lonely, not often anyway. The loneliest times were the walks to school. I'd set off down the long hill and past Johnson Elementary School where my Mother taught fourth grade. I watched the gangs of kids forming up along the route to Saint James Catholic School, girls giggling together, their heads conspiratorially close, trading magazines and hairstyles and the gossip about teen idols or boys in class. I passed the same landmarks every day, there's the street to my other grandparent's house, there's where Bobby D'Orio lives, (He's so dreamy!) there's Mary Fiorentino's house, I wonder if she'll walk to school with me one day? Sometimes some of the girls would let me accompany them but more often, I walked alone every morning and afternoon. In seventh grade, there was a girl named Denise, a beautiful, popular girl, and a cheerleader for the grade school basketball team. We sometimes walked in each other's vicinity back and forth to school. One afternoon in the stairwell of the school, Denise approached me.

"Would you like to be friends with me?"

"Yes! I'd love to!" I was thrilled beyond my wildest dreams.

"OK, we can be friends, but just don't tell anyone. I don't want anyone else to know"

"Don't worry, I won't tell anyone."

"I've got to go, let me go out first so nobody sees us together." She went out the door and left me there confused.

"OK, Denise, whatever you say."

I was so sadly longing for friends, I accepted this.

To this day, I wonder as to her motivation. We were friends in a casual sort of way, talked on the phone sometimes and went to each other's homes, but it didn't last long. It may have been the fact that I got good grades, and she needed someone to help her with homework, it may have been catholic conscience coming home to her.

Most of the girls I went around with lived close to me, and they drifted in and out of my life, thick as thieves one moment and distant the next. We had slumber parties, afternoon homework sessions, and as we grew older, talks about boys and music, all the usual girl things. But there was always a distance for me, a sense of being an invader into their pretty bedrooms, their normal families. I was the only child in my class from a single parent home. I was overweight, wore glasses, and was abnormally intelligent. And that odd sense of humor that I inherited from my family set me across a canyon of understanding from the rest of the kids. They were cruel, as they are today to anyone different; this is as eternal as Rome. I like to believe that it made me a stronger person, and I have no doubt that it did in some ways build character. But I would have given anything for one day of total acceptance.

Holidays were magic. The three-arched porch exchanged its canvas awnings for bright teardrops of blue and red and all the colors of the rainbow. Smaller lights framed the windows and twinkled like so many glossy snowflakes. A red felt sign with hanging jingle bells proclaimed "Noel" on the heavy oak front door, and the bells in their gay voices announced guests and family coming and going. An elf clung to the small chandelier in the front hall, a bell in his belly and mistletoe on his feet. The greeting cards hung from a gilt thread around the arch to the living room, and the tree stood in the corner, ablaze with lights. The decorations and ornaments of the season are so ingrained on my memories; they come to life every year again when I place them in my home. The tree stood a good seven feet tall, artificial, but lovely. A gleaming metallic star, lined with multicolored lights, sat atop the tree and what seemed like thousands of ornaments nestled in its branches. The ornaments ran the gamut from child-made to store bought, from antique to new. Fragile glass balls with bits of fluff inside, dusted with a snow like paint in a holiday theme, a set of beaded ornaments that framed family photographs, each one different and wonderful. I loved the ornaments. I gazed at them for hours on end, wondering at their fragile beauty, at the stories behind each one. A train ran under the tree, and somewhere among the tracks was the nativity set. It was one of the stranger ones I have ever seen. Mismatched pieces, different styles, sizes and colors. Mary sat before a crib that held a baby Jesus the same size as her. Joseph larger than Mary, but still not large enough to hold this fantastic progeny in the crib. Sheep ranging from tiny to gargantuan, some as large as the camel that accompanied the Magi, some smaller than the flask of myrrh that one King held. I loved this set. Its origins were unknown to me, but I knew there had to be a tale there to tell. One piece from one source, two from another. And here came the train, chugging past the representation of ancient Bethlehem.

I had trouble sleeping Christmas Eve, as any child would. For one thing, Christmas Eve was when the family all gathered at the house and exchanged gifts. The relatives came from everywhere, all the cousins, aunts, uncles, filling the house with love. There were so many of them, more than I can recall now. This was the best day of the entire year, as far as I was concerned. Smoke and laughter filled the house. My Pap even seemed happy on Christmas Eve. Gram was in her glory, her cooking weighing the table and sideboard and even the coffee table. She baked and cooked for weeks preparing for this day. Seven Fish, according to tradition, plus home made cookies and cakes and pastries, salads and side dishes, bread and biscuits. And the pasta, in a huge steaming bowl covered with cheese, the smell filling the house. Gram, Non, and Aunt Mary made the pasta and the baked goods on the kitchen table. Weeks before Christmas, as the advent candles were lit one by one, the cooking was done. Wand, a wonderful Italian fried cookie, cut and twisted from sheets of dough and dusted with powdered sugar. Stroufolli, little balls of the same dough fried and drizzled with honey and then topped with sprinkles and little silver sugar balls. Pizza Fiatta, an amazing nut roll, the most treasured delicacy, filled with nuts and chocolate chips and citron and dried pineapple, topped again with honey and sprinkles. More varieties of cookies and pies and cakes than could be imagined, even in the wildest dreams of a food-loving child like myself. The pasta was also rolled out and cut on the kitchen table. Aunt Mary seemed to be the authority on this process. She was a very old woman, her arms huge and hanging soft flesh, her face deeply creased. She wasn't a blood relative, but rather a widowed in-law of a Fusco cousin. Her house, where we sometimes visited, was on a street named Gas Alley. You entered through the back, directly into the kitchen. It seemed her kitchen was the largest room in the house. It was also upstairs; the bedrooms of the house were on the ground floor, which accessed the main street. Across the alley from her house was a vacant lot where my Gram went in the spring to pick dandelion leaves. She used them in salads, or cooked them as greens. If taken before flowering, they are sweet and delicious.

If we were fortunate enough to catch Aunt Mary early enough in the day, we would find her with her hair down. It was thick, wavy, and reached almost to the back of her knees. It was beautiful, intertwining strands of black and grey and white. She did it up in a braid, then coiled the braid atop her head and fixed it with pins. Her ankles were thicker than anyone's I had ever seen, thick to the point that they hung slightly over her solid black shoes. She spoke heavily accented English, and seemed to prefer speaking Italian when she could. Aunt Mary was a master at forming pasta and pizza out of the clay of fresh dough. She and my Gram and Non stood over the kitchen table, with cutters and rollers and all sorts of tools at the ready, arms working, smiling, aprons fixed carefully over flowered dresses, flour everywhere. I loved watching them, almost as much as I loved the fruits of their labor. I think the love and the gossip and the spice of the communal effort was what made the food so delicious.

Early in the evening Christmas Eve, the family would begin to arrive. One at a time, like small bunches of grapes that made up the vine, they arrived with gifts and food and hugs and kisses and warm holiday greetings. The gifts were piled according to the recipient under the tree. The women went to the kitchen to talk and laugh and discuss children and grandchildren and husbands, the men sat in the dining room with drinks or wine or coffee and discussed sports and politics and wives. The teenagers and young adults went to the rumpus room or sat in the living room. For most of these years, I was the only child in the family. I went from one group to the next, watching, listening, asking questions, tasting food, and rattling packages to guess at the contents. There was never a formal sit-down meal, just an endless bountiful buffet. When the time arrived, the gifts would be distributed, oldest to youngest and opened with a great display of oohs and aahs and admiration. There was never silence. We were a very loud bunch. The men and women alike had deep booming voices and laughter that carried up and down the street. Jokes or arguments carried the same volume. At some point in the festivities, someone would begin singing;

"Tu scendi dalle stellae,
O re del cielo
Vieni in una grotta
Al freddo e al gelo
Vieni in una grotta
Al freddo e al gelo"
(You came down from the stars
King of heaven
Born into a little cave
In the cold and ice
Born into a little cave
In the cold and ice)

The carol "O Bambino" brings those warm happy days into my mind fresh and sharp and fragrant, all the childlike hopes and dreams intact, the rust and jading of the years gone and forgotten. Another miracle of Christmas, another miracle of love. Not all the voices were beautiful, but most were, and all could carry a tune well. We harmonized and strained and made up forgotten words. It was the most wonderful of all the choirs I ever sang in. It was meant.

After the family kissed and hugged and said goodnight, I was sent off to bed. I practically crawled up the staircase, looking wistfully over the gracefully shining wooden rails, catching my last glimpses of the tree and the lights and the leavings of the evening. Disappearing around the corner, clutching a new favorite toy or book or doll, followed close by my Mother or Gram, I went to bed regretfully and with anticipation for the new joys that morning would bring. I usually got a bedtime story, and after the designated relative would leave the room, I'd gaze out at the window, at the stars, or at the stellar flakes of softly falling snow, and dream memories and wishes. I listened for sleigh bells, watched for the red gleam of Rudolph's nose in the sky, and drifted off content.

Christmas morning, it seems there was always snow. The dim and silent morning found me stealing down the stairs in the cool white predawn glow. Three steps then a triangular landing where I would pause and gather myself for the surprises to be found. Around the corner and the first sight of the bounty under the tree, and the stockings stuffed to the limit. Mine was the biggest. There was candy, small toys, endless things to look at and touch, and inevitably, a net sack of gold wrapped coin shaped chocolates. An orange was always in the toe, to fill it out and provide a possible nutritious base for the treats above.

Christmas day was a quieter day, after breakfast, the presents were opened, and it seemed there was always snow to go out and play in. We went to mass, if we had not gone to midnight services the night before, and came home to explore the new presents then go to Non and Aunt Anna's house for the evening. My grandmother packed up an enormous amount of leftovers and goodies from the night before to take along. It was a calming, peaceful day, one to bask in the love and generosity of the family.

When I was fifteen years old, my Gram suffered a series of heart attacks. She lingered for two weeks before finally passing out of this world from her bed in the Veteran's Administration Hospital. They played "Taps" at her funeral, and carefully folded the flag from her coffin into a regulation triangle before handing it to my Pap. We were devastated that this rock had eroded. She was gone, the unstoppable Fran, the strongest person I ever knew. My Pap continued living in the house at 1420 Franklin until he died as well, three years later, from cancer and loneliness and aimless drifting.

I have driven past the house many times. I still smell and taste and feel the happiness and sadness of a child when I see the archways, the porch, the rust brick and crank-out windows. I wonder if the people there are happy. I hope they are. The house held much love for many years; it could not help but pass some of it on.

729 Ardmore Boulevard

If any child were given a choice about what house to spend the weekends of their youth, 729 Ardmore Boulevard would have to be it. A huge, rambling place, rooms without end, corners that a child could hide in for hours and never be found but for the beckoning of the heavenly smells issuing forth from the kitchen. My maiden aunts lived here, in the ancestral homestead of the Fusco family. The house sits on a busy street, which is part of State Route 30. The trucks and cars whizzed by at all hours of the day and night, and the battle for the cleanliness of the porch was never ending. I imagine what the house must have been like when my great-grandparents moved into it. The neighborhood must have been very different then.

You walked up the three steps that led to a short landing before another three steps to the porch. The front yard was tiny, and framed by the same yellow brick that covered the house. There were a few flower bushes of unknown origin there, perhaps azaleas, perhaps hydrangeas, perhaps something else. The porch was large and comfortable, but completely bare of any furniture. Entering the front door, there was an enormous foyer with the stairs to the right and the living room to the left. This was the warmest house of my childhood, not in terms of temperature but rather of atmosphere. Aunt Non and Aunt Anna lived there. They were the unmarried sisters of my Grandmother, as different as night and day but alike in their capacity for spoiling a great-niece.

Photographs hung on the walls and were set into albums that gave clues to the world of their youth. As a child, I wondered, as many children do, if the world was sepia-toned then. Strange and familiar faces alike, a graduation portrait of a cousin who passed away at an early age, her beauty frozen, forever seventeen and perfect. A long formally posed photograph of the Fusco family, incomplete. The parents, my grandmother a babe in arms, Uncle Larry, and Aunt Non. There was another child there, one I didn't know. It was my Aunt Rose, the eldest daughter. She succumbed to the scarlet fever epidemic in 1918, at the age of 11 or 12. They are unsmiling, grim in the photo. I wondered if they had such miserable lives. It was many years later while studying photography that I learned they had to sit still for long periods of time while the film was exposed. It made smiling difficult. The faces are the same, though. I see my mother and myself and my children looking out at me from dark eyes perched above prominent noses. The intelligence beaming out of their faces is the same.

    I spent many hours in wonderment at the photos in the albums. They were a well-traveled bunch, the Fuscos. There are pages and pages of photographs of the family all over the country, from Pike's Peak to Atlantic City, posed smiling in front of improbable cars, shops and landmarks. They had a lot of fun.

    Every new arrival to the family was documented with photographs taken in the miniscule backyard on Ardmore. From my Mother to myself, each baby was done up and snapped there. Alone, and in the company of relatives, with toys and without, and at every occasion from baptism to first communion to confirmation, the moment was memorialized. There are plenty of casual shots too; they must have spent an enormous amount of money on film and processing. They were the precursors of the current trend, if you don't record an event, how do you know it actually happened? If camcorders had existed then, they would have had one. As it was, somewhere in the house were an old 8mm-movie projector, a screen, and stacks of films. These were somewhat more modern, but had the sepia tone feel of history.

    The rooms in the house were enormous. The furnishings were old but tasteful and most are now treasured antiques in the homes of various family. Again, the dining room was the center of life. The dining room table was like an indoor jungle gym to a small child. Heavy Mediterranean style furniture, the table capable of seating ten adults before extending the leaves. I lived in this house as an infant, my mother and father and I with the Aunts. My father was gone before I could form a memory of him, though, and at a very young age my mother and I moved in with Gram and Pap. But I spent every weekend in my childhood at 729 Ardmore Boulevard. The house itself was utterly fascinating. Three stories, huge windows with old-fashioned wooden Venetian blinds. The basement was unfinished and cavernous. Rickety wooden stairs with a head-threatening ledge after the third step, they led into a bare cement floor that was surely dirt in the not too distant past. Right at the bottom of the stairs were 2 doors, one leading to a coal cellar and the other to a mystery called a "root cellar". Whether or not there were actual roots there, I have no idea. An ancient wringer washer stood in the center of the floor, insurance against the day that the modern appliances against the wall stopped working. I rode my tricycle around it in circles watching Non do the laundry many times.

Aunt Non was the single biggest influence in my life. Her real name was Nellie but one of my cousins changed it in his baby talk to Non, and it stuck. My grandmother was the head of the family, but Non was its heart. The same height as my Gram, she was half again as broad. A round, warm, smiling woman with kind eyes and an unlined face, she was always perfectly beautiful to me. Non was the youngest sister of the Fuscos. Looking now at photographs of her as a young woman, I can see that she was not an attractive girl, heavy with thick legs and a broad face, but still her beauty of spirit is there. She was completely indulgent of all her nieces and nephews, and as the first grandniece, I was again especially loved. I never realized how fortunate I was to be the darling of all these warm, wonderful, generous people. She worked hard all her life, and when she came home from work, her domain was the kitchen. As wonderful a cook as my Grandmother was, Non put her in the shade. Maybe it was the house, and the proximity to the souls of the first generation Italian immigrants that her parents were, but I have never tasted anything like her cooking. She was patient to a fault with my questions. Non always had time to listen to me, time to play a game, time to talk. She never tired of telling stories about the family and her parents, and she never tired of arguing with Aunt Anna about the facts versus the fiction in these stories. I didn't care. I loved to hear them talk, to hear the love in their voices buried under the sisterly bickering. I longed for a sister then.

"Non, tell me about when Frankie got in trouble for taking Uncle Larry's car."

"Well, it was 1957, Frankie was 12 years old and Larry had just bought that new Buick"

"Nell, you know darn well it was an Oldsmobile!"

"No it wasn't, Ann, it was a Buick, I remember. It was a big sedan."

"No it wasn't a sedan, Nellie, it was a coupe with a rumble seat. Can't you get anything right?"

"Oh Ann you're the one that cant get anything right. It was a sedan, do you think Virg would have let him get a coupe with all those kids?"

"I know it was a coupe just like I know my own name, Nell."

"Then you don't know your name too well, Ann!"

"Why do you always have to argue with me, Nellie?"

"Why do you always have to contradict me, Ann? I wasn't even talking to you to begin with; I was talking to Jamie. Madonna Mia, you can't mind your own business."

"When you tell a story about the family wrong, Nell, that is my business. Don't you think she deserves to get the truth instead of your make-believe?"

At this point, they usually began speaking Italian to each other. I didn't know what most of the words meant but if I repeated them later, I got in big trouble.

Friday afternoons, Gram would take me in the car to pick up Non or Aunt Anna and off to the grocery store we went. We usually went to 2 different stores, the A&P and the Kroger's. Gram was a bargain hunter, and she knew where the best prices were to be found at all times. We spent an hour or two shopping, bags and bags of food to take home, shopping for

2 households at once and managing to get it all in the trunk of Gram's Impala, Franklin Avenue bags on one side, Ardmore Boulevard bags on the other. She would drop me and whichever Aunt had accompanied us at 729 Ardmore, and leave me there. That's how weekends usually began.

My Aunts and their siblings had grown up during the depression. They were completely generous, but were appalled by waste of any kind. They had a thousand tricks to stretch a meal, to make the groceries go further. After the shopping expedition was complete and the things put away, Aunt Anna would cover the kitchen table with newspaper and Non would pour a bag of freshly ground 8 'O Clock coffee on it. They mixed the coffee with chicory to stretch it out, and then placed it in the canister to stay fresh. The fragrance of the fresh ground coffee was wonderful, and the chicory added an edge to it, a unique and unforgettable smell. The kitchen itself wasn't terribly large but had ample counters and opened onto the back porch. The back yard was as tiny as the front, with a wrought iron fence around the back to prevent falling off the steep hillside onto the alley behind Franklin Avenue below. There was a gate and stairs leading down to a garage set in the alley, a garage that was never used that I can recall. In the corner of the yard were a sour cherry tree and a small patch of mint. A lax clothesline went from one corner of the yard to the other, and when laundry was hung there, the prop poles came from the back of the basement doors to hold the clean sheets off the ground. The back porch was bare concrete with no railing, with a few chairs set around. In spite of its small size, the yard was a fun place. There was a mysterious cavern beneath the back porch, long dark walkways between the adjoining houses, and a good variety of plants and insects to investigate. A large window in the kitchen overlooked the yard, and there was a spectacular view of the neighborhoods across on the other hillside. Wilkinsburg is all hills, with small sub-neighborhoods nestled among them, lines drawn depending on the angle of the hill, the curve of the street, or the end of the buildable terrain. It's a scenic place, spectacular in fall and very sleddable in winter. We had a family member or friend in most of these neighborhoods, and none were too terribly far apart. The view of the houses perched in an unlikely fashion on the hills across was a wondrous sight from Non's kitchen. The kitchen itself was white tiled, sunny and immaculately clean. It was also carpeted, somewhat of an oddity in those days. The kitchen was not used for guest meals as a rule, with one exception. Uncle Joe came to visit every Saturday morning. He brought a box of Danish or doughnuts and we sat in the kitchen with him and talked. You could set your watch by Uncle Joe, rain or shine; he was there every Saturday at 9am sharp. We never visited him or his wife and children, though we sometimes saw them at weddings or funerals or holidays. Never with the frequency of the other uncles and their wives and children, though. In fact, when I was almost grown, it became habit among the cousins of my Mother's generation to refer to Aunt Mary as the "myth". Years later, I learned there had been an argument, accusations and resentments between Mary and my Gram, or perhaps it was Aunt Anna. It was enough to eternally divide the family, but not enough to keep Uncle Joe from his beloved sisters. Joe was the baby of the Fusco siblings. He was a jolly round-headed man, mostly bald and always smiling. He smoked a wonderfully fragrant pipe. Uncle Joe was generous and loving. He never had a cross word for me, and was never empty handed around any child. Whether it was a coin or a butterscotch candy or a stick of teaberry gum, he always had something to give. When I was small, he brought me a doll that was easily twice my size. According to my Mother, he won it in a raffle, and rather than take the cash prize, or the basket of cheer, he chose the doll for me. He said he wanted to make sure I had a doll for Christmas. It was one of those "walking" dolls in a Dutch costume. I don't remember the actual Christmas involved, I think I was too young, but I do remember the doll. It was wonderful. When I was older, I managed to remove the head and one of the arms, and was amazed to discover the complex system of rubber bands that made her walk. But I never could get her put back together properly. Uncle Joe and Non and Aunt Anna had a special closeness. They would sit in the kitchen and talk and drink coffee from Non's stainless steel drip pot with the scents from the chicory blend and the pipe filling the air. These days were a constant, something that could be depended upon not to change. Years later, when they were very old and Non lived in a senior citizens' home, Uncle Joe still came every Saturday, at 9am sharp, pastries in hand, though he had abandoned the pipe in the interest of his health long before. Back in Non's kitchen, though, the smoke circled their heads along with the talk of family, friends, and memories. They almost never argued. And Aunt Anna never argued when Uncle Joe was there either. He was a calming, peace-making influence on them.

The entire family was deeply religious. We attended Mass every Sunday, every obligatory Holy Day, confession every Friday, and observed meatless Fridays, not just during Lent, but every Friday. The first time I visited a friend and was served meat on a Friday for dinner, I had no idea what to do. If I ate it, I would have to return home with the guilt of having done something obviously terribly wrong. If I declined, I risked offending my friend's Mother. As I didn't have very many friends, I couldn't take that risk. But the guilt on returning home and being questioned about what was served was almost unbearable.

Aunt Anna was the most devout of the family. I used to think she was a Nun that had received permission to live at home. She usually wore a black dress, stout black shoes and nylons. She wore a crucifix over her dress at all times, and a scapular under. She was short, as all the Fuscos were, and quite trim. She had a lovely and expressive face, the same wonderful eyes behind her glasses. When I saw photos of her as a young woman, I marveled at the difference between the stern woman I knew and the achingly beautiful girl she was. Her hair was white, thick, and wavy. Her features were regular, her mouth small and bowed, and her nose a muted version of my Gram's. When I spent the weekend there, I slept with Aunt Anna. She had crucifixes hanging in various places around her room, and decorating her dresser and vanity and nightstand along with the photos of family and friends and places she had been. There was a ceramic Holy Water font fixed to the doorway of her room. She was a telephone operator, and after she retired, she traveled extensively, to Rome, to

Lourdes, to Guadeloupe, and even to the Holy Land. It seemed there wasn't a religious shrine in the western hemisphere that she hadn't seen. She held her faith like a torch, and at times like a weapon. I was in terror sometimes of her Jesus, but I loved her. One of her favorite religious mementos was what I perceived as a Catholic first aid kit. It hung on the wall, a lovely wooden box, shaped into a cross with the painted Jesus on it. If you removed the cover and put it aside (after, of course, kissing the painted feet) you saw a candle, a bottle of Holy Water, and a small tin of the sacred oil known as chrism. Aunt Anna explained to me that in an emergency, someone not of the priesthood could perform the last rites on a dying person, or baptize a dying infant using this kit. It was a wonder to me. I could very easily imagine Aunt Anna rushing to the scene of an accident, cruciform box in hand, to administer the final anointing to the hapless victims. It suited her to be so prepared.

Aunt Anna was a very clean person, but she had her own concepts about what was particularly despised. Her worst enemies were the pigeons that roosted in the eaves of the house. I didn't mind them, I loved all living things then as I do now, and I didn't understand Aunt Anna's contempt for the pigeons. When she cleaned, one of her chores was to open the window on the third floor of the house and sweep the nests and the eggs within them to the ground below. I watched in dismay as the progeny of these innocent birds was destroyed, at least once a month. I liked the pigeons, admired their iridescent feathers and their personality as they strutted and cooed around the back yard. Some of them I even named. But Aunt Anna hated them. "Dirty birds!" she would exclaim, as she swept the nests off the ledge beneath the eaves. "They're just like rats!" She wasn't a vicious person; she just hated the pigeons. And I loved her, so I didn't hold her at fault for her hatred.

When I was about 9 years old, our existence at that house was changed, irrevocably. An old friend of the family, John Diana, came to town. He rang the bell at 729 Ardmore and when I saw him, I knew that our pleasant, complacent reality was over. John was a dapper, dashing, utterly charming man in his early sixties. Aunt Anna, at that time, was about 62. She and John had been childhood sweethearts. They had loved each other completely in that childlike innocence when they were 15 and 17, respectively. John was somewhat of a playboy, however, and family legend takes different paths at this point in the story. The more conservative version had John asking for Anna's hand in marriage and being refused. His reputation as a rake made him unacceptable for the eldest Fusco daughter. He then moved to California out of heartbreak. The second version, the one I prefer, is rather more risqué. John Diana was very handsome, very charming, a real sweet talker. He was this even in his sixties and seventies, when I knew him as my Uncle. As a young man, though, stories have it that he had gotten a girl of good and connected family "in trouble". In the 1920's, in Italian neighborhoods, your choices in such a predicament were rather limited. He had the option to marry her, or die at the hands of her relatives. He chose to flee to California.

He married a woman there, raised children and grandchildren, and enjoyed a good life. When his wife passed away, he came back to Wilkinsburg to see Aunt Anna. Her love for him had not diminished one bit in almost half a century, and neither had his for her. He visited one afternoon, chaperoned by Non, and had dinner with us. The next day, he presented himself to my Uncle Nick, the eldest of the family, and asked for Anna's hand in marriage. They were married about a month later in Las Vegas, and Aunt Anna moved to his California home. The family was stunned but happy for them. There were many undercurrents of discontent that I sensed at the time, but dismissed. I thought it was my begrudging Aunt Anna her long-awaited happiness. It turned out to be much deeper than that.

Aunt Anna and Uncle John had a very happy and loving marriage. They traveled the world together, always off on a cruise to exotic places. They belonged to dancing groups, singing ensembles, and AARP together. They had 25 blissful years. John's children and grandchildren treated her like their mother, like their grandmother. They were hers just as surely as he was. When he passed away, in the 25th year of their marriage, she stayed on in their California home and then in a senior's home in the same area. His children looked after her, and she passed away 3 years later. I saw her the summer before she died. She was happy, smiling, and content in her faith that she would be with her beloved John soon. The following March, she joined him. Some of the family went to California to the funeral, and when they returned, we arranged a memorial service and luncheon for the rest. The church where the service was held is modern, and has a skylight set into the roof. We all sat and sang and prayed and remembered Aunt Anna. After communion, I looked up and saw a pigeon in the skylight. Realizing that they are doves at heart, I knew that Aunt Anna was watching us there, knowing how we loved her. I felt that she had learned to love the pigeons at last, and returned to that skylight in that form to feel the love of her family one more time.

After the memorial, Non spoke to me about her feelings. She was 86 years old then, but still lucid.

"How are you doing, Non?" I asked her, leaning down to her so that she could hear me. She was now a tiny woman, frail. She was mostly deaf and about three-fourths blind.

"I'm ok, Jamie. I just wish I could cry."

"You should cry, Non. It's good for you." Non was now the last of the Fusco siblings. I could only imagine her loneliness, her pain.

"I want to, but I can't!" Her face was full of grief, emotion, but her eyes were dry. "I haven't cried since Mom died. I don't know what's wrong with me."

"I'm sorry, Non, I don't know what to say." I held her hand and stroked the back of it absently, while I tried to think of how I could diminish her pain, or at least make it easier for her to bear.

"You know, I can feel the tears there. My eyes are full of tears. But I can't make them come out, no matter what I do."

I had enough tears for the both of us. Not only for Aunt Anna's passing, but also for the pain and frustration that Non was feeling. I've always been able to cry, sometimes too easily. It was beyond my comprehension to have a need for tears and be unable to produce them. But in my life with and away from my family, I had learned that things were not so idyllic as they seemed. There was a great deal of manipulation in our family, a great deal of guilt and psychological game playing. There was tremendous love, but it seemed it was so hard for them to express it in a healthy manner. A short time after that, I learned what led to the feelings of disquiet I had sensed when Aunt Anna married.

My great grandmother, Josephine, was a mystery to me. She had died long before I was born, but she lived among her children all along. It seemed her influence was greatest with Non and Aunt Anna, that they, living in her house, were closest to her shade. It came up in a conversation I had with my mother that Josephine had exacted a deathbed promise from Non and Aunt Anna, separately and without the other's knowledge, to look after each other for life, no matter what. That was why they had never married, and that was the reason for the discontent when Aunt Anna reconciled her need for happiness against that unreasonable request, so much later, having spent her life doing what her mother said to do. Non was never able to get past the manipulation of that promise. She never got the chance to break away from her mother and live. It seems so reprehensible now, but I suppose that it was her only way of making certain her girls were safe. She did the only thing she knew to do, locked them together with all the strength of their love, guilt, and obligation to their family. Non could no longer look after her sister when she married, and Aunt Anna couldn't take care of Non from afar, no matter how much she wanted to. She had resolved to be happy as she could, but the guilt remained with her. Neither one of them truly broke away from that promise, from that manipulation.

Non had a very long memory for unpleasant things. In a house that had 5 bedrooms, she slept in the tiniest room there, probably the room that had been hers as a child. She never slept without an open window, no matter how cold, no matter how windy or rainy or snowy. We accepted that as just the way she was, but there was a reason. When she was a teenager, in February of 1936, an entire branch of the Fusco family had perished in a coal furnace malfunction. Father, Mother and three children aged 21, 18, and 13 years succumbed to the carbon monoxide fumes the same day. The 17-year-old daughter lived eight days, and then died. This was a tragedy of such a magnitude that the grief lasts even into my generation. I have a Mass card from their funeral. The inscription at the top reads "We have loved them during life. Let us not abandon them until we have conducted them by our prayers into the house of the Lord." Non never abandoned their memory.

Her room must have been a nursery at one time; it was a tiny room set off the master bedroom. It had her narrow single bed, a night table, a large closet, and a chest of drawers. No room for anything else. A door led from her room into the hall and a second door into the master bedroom. In the hall stood a wonderful cedar chest, with legs, doors, a drawer in the bottom, and a clock set into the back. There were always interesting things in there for a child to look through, play with, and discover. That cedar chest now sits in my dining room and is still packed with wonders. To the right was the staircase, and to the left the door to the master bedroom, the room that Aunt Anna and I shared. Then the stairs to the third floor, and finally another bedroom on the left. At the very end of the hall was a kitchen that was installed when my mother and father and I lived there. It was never used now, but stood there completely functional. On the right was a bathroom, remarkably done in pink and black, a deco masterpiece. It wasn't a large bathroom, but it was adequate and the colors were wonderful. If you went up the stairs to the third floor, there were two enormous bedrooms, one on either side. They were cavernous and made more so by the sloping ceilings above. They held old dusty furniture, trunks, and the smell of rooms long left empty. On the bed in the front bedroom was a doll. This doll had moving eyes, arms and legs, a pretty though faded dress, and scant blonde hair. It had been a childhood toy of one of the girls, and was the only one I ever saw. I wasn't allowed to play with it as such, but I would look at it, or stroke its flaxen hair, and imagine that it was mine, that the life it had shared was mine. What I, at that time, perceived as a normal life, with father and mother both, sisters and brothers. I imagined they were happy. I suppose they were, or as close to it as was possible. I look on my wall now and see the photograph of the Fusco family, mother and father and 6 children. They are smiling, close together and posed impeccably in the back yard of the house at 729 Ardmore Blvd, an ideal family in an idealistic age. I see myself there, my mother and my children, all reflected in the dreams and hopes in their eyes.

After Aunt Anna married and moved away, Non and I continued to share weekends together. We would board a bus every Saturday morning and ride the half-hour or so into downtown Pittsburgh. Once there, we would go to Kaufmann's department store, then to Lane Bryant's, then to lunch at Palmer's or Woolworth's. After lunch, we went to a movie. I preferred the lunch at Woolworth's because you got to pop a balloon and pay the price on the slip of paper inside for a banana split. Non was very indulgent. She bought me things, took me places, and loved me more, I thought, than anyone else. I believed then, and still believe now, that every family should have a Non, someone to spoil and indulge nieces and nephews.

In the evenings after our shopping trips, we came home, had dinner, and settled in to watch television. Non would sit in her chair next to the ancient Victrola cabinet, and I would sit at her feet, wondering at her bunions and corns and the price she paid for the years of standing on her feet. She worked as a janitor for Rockwell. All those years of work had sentenced her to orthopedic shoes and pain, but she never complained about it. She simply took her shoes off, rolled her stockings down to her knees, and put her feet up on the hassock with a sigh of relief. Sometimes we lay on the couch to watch TV, Non with her head on the cushions and me tucked in behind her legs, my head on her hip. We watched an endless succession of programs, years and years of changing Saturday night fare. From Ed Sullivan, to Andy Williams, from Petticoat Junction to Love American Style, the programs and the years ran together. Non was especially fond of situation comedies and variety shows. She didn't care much for dramas except for one or two soap operas in the daytime. Saturday nights were ours, and they were spent in the living room. There was a wonderful mantelpiece, made of some grey and singularly unyielding stone, that was only equipped for a gas burning heater. The little valve in the cave of the mantel was never hooked to anything, and I am not sure if it was ever used. The overhanging piece had very sharp corners. I think there are dents in my head to attest to that fact even today. It had a garland of ivy carved into it, and was deep and high enough to make a cavern for my imagination. My toys had their residence inside the fireplace there, and when I played, the toys came out and I went in. The cool ceramic floor was perfect for cars and Barbie houses and the tiny wooden train set I had. I spent hours playing in that recess.

The house had large archways between the rooms on the first floor, rather than doorways. From the foyer to the living room and from the living room to the dining room with its enormous dark furniture, and the memories of all the joyful hours spent at family gatherings there. It was a very warm room. An ancient treadle sewing machine stood on the right hand wall, and the china cabinet on the left. There was usually some sort of centerpiece on the table, dried flowers, or plastic fruit, which would be moved to the sideboard for meals and games of dominoes or penny-ante poker. The family loved games. Dominoes were a particular favorite. Uncle Larry and Uncle Nick, Non and Aunt Anna, or Gram, or Uncle Joe would pull out the set of black and white double-sixes, form teams, and play game after game. I learned domino strategy along with my ABC's, was fed scoring rules with mother's milk. I love the game to this day; it stands second only to chess for me. I never forgot the associations of dots, the best tiles to have, the rows upon rows of Xs forming the score, five rows of five and the game was over. Uncle Larry was the oldest brother. He was a short, round man, bald on top, with a white circle of hair from ear to ear cropped short in the back. He was a barber with a shop down the street from Non and Aunt Anna's house. He was a rather gruff man, but loving in his own way. His house was the place we held New Year's Eve celebrations. He smoked enormous cigars, vile smelling things that announced his arrival from a good quarter mile. Uncle Larry and Aunt Gina had 4 sons. They were practically adults by the time I was born, but still cousins more like brothers to me. Uncle Nick was the tallest of the Fuscos. He was a good-looking man, his hair not completely faded to grey and a thick black moustache. Uncle Nick also smoked cigars and the occasional pipe, though his cigars seemed less offensive than the ones Larry smoked. Christmas afternoon was designated for Uncle Nick's house. Nick and Aunt Ruth had a son and a daughter, in the same age group as my mother and Uncle Larry's boys. Uncle Joe had a son and a daughter as well, but we didn't see them any more than we saw his wife, the elusive Aunt Mary. Joe's son, Fred, was ordained a priest when I was around 10 years old. The pride in the whole family, and particularly in Uncle Joe, was so great it was like a shimmering light on us all. Freddie was incredibly intelligent, deeply spiritual. I remember his ordination, the white-cassocked young men lying on their faces before the altar, giving their lives completely to the church. Freddie's first mass is also vivid to me; he was brilliantly clad in Pentecostal green, his handsome face transfixed in spiritual fulfillment. Uncle Joe had tears in his eyes. Some years later, Freddie left the priesthood. That shimmer changed to a dark cloud to all the family, except Uncle Joe. He simply loved his child and accepted his decision. When Freddie brought his new wife, Judy, to meet the family, all was ice, except in Uncle Joe's heart. He made her welcome, embraced her as his daughter, and respected her for the love his son had found in her. None of his sisters and brothers understood, and I am not certain Uncle Joe understood either. He simply loved. His heart was truly generous.

729 Ardmore Boulevard stands vacant and dilapidated now. It is in one of the worst parts of town, a situation that is not helped by being on a main road and having no place to park. I grieve for the house, for the memories and the love and the ghosts that probably reside there still. The

day the house was sold was an agony for me. I'm certain I was not alone in that agony.

Driving past the house, I wonder if the granite mantelpiece remains, if the sour cherry tree stands in the back yard still, if the pigeons roost in peace in the eaves. That would be some small consolation, a tiny fragment of the happiest times of my life.

The Magic Gift

Noon, and a knock on the door.

I open the door to find a large box, taped within an inch of its life, and the UPS truck pulling away. I had no idea what to expect, only that there was a package on the way. The box is larger than I expected; I can't imagine what might be inside. Back in the house for a knife. The tape looks very strong.

Hoist the box on top of the peacock chair that sits on the porch, wow, it's heavy! I begin to hack away with the knife, sawing at layer upon layer of tape. The tempting nature of the package is proportionate to the difficulty of opening. At last, an opening appears.

The last few days have been so hard, and I have felt so bad about my life and myself in general, that it seems nothing can bring me out of the blue fog that surrounds me. The first glimpse in the box reveals another box. No clue. I continue sawing away at the tape, and then begin ripping it away from the box in frustration. *What* is in here? The first opened, then a round of fresh sawing at the second box. I wonder if I'll have to contend with an endless line of boxes, smaller and smaller 'til I reach an envelope containing a fax. No, it's too heavy. At last, an opening. Corn shucks? Maybe packing material. No, its Indian corn, I know it. Indian corn to hang on the door for the harvest season. I feel the first prickling of tears behind my eyes; I can sense the depth of meaning that will be contained in this simple cardboard. Remove and admire the corn, then amazed, I look into the box. Not a scrap of packing material. Its full of things, so many things I am totally stunned and have to step back. My eyes fog over.

Gourds. Beautiful, colorful gourds. I admire them one by one and set them on the porch ledge. The first tears come out of my eyes, and I am murmuring words, I don't know what to say, but I am saying things like "I cant believe" and "this is incredible" and "what a wonderful thing!" There are small pumpkins there too, I smile wondering where these number among the three thousand, and I am crying and laughing at once. A gift for the season.

Books. Read, worn books, the most precious kind. The kind that have known eyes, known appreciation, and have earned passing on to a friend. A gift for the mind, the imagination.

One book is different; it is bound in soft leather and tied with a thong. I open it, fumbling at the knot, barely able to see what I am doing through the tears. A simple note, and creamy blank pages. Sobbing now, I run my finger over the words written inside the cover, and I have to step back a moment, holding the silky leather against my face, marking it already with tears of amazement and happiness. A gift for creativity, for my spirit.

There's a CD there, I am overwhelmed. For the ears, the soul. I know before I even look at it that it will be calming, joyful music.

More pumpkins, they line up alongside the gourds, six in all, one for each living being in my home. I pull the largest one from the box, disturbing a bunch of bags that can only contain bulbs. I laugh and cry more, a gift for the future, for forever. A gift that will come in spring, early and late, to remind me of this day. Tulips, Daffodils, and a wonderful Amaryllis. Indoor and outdoor, now and later, living gifts. So precious.

I see the neck of a bottle of wine among the bags and books. It's wrapped in red fabric. I lift it, knowing what it is, smiling at the promise I never expected to see fulfilled, knowing I can share this across the country, a gift for the taste.

The red fabric falls away, and I can see it's a shirt, with a wonderful scent emanating from it. I hold it to my face, soft, and inhale deeply. It's wonderful. He wore this, I think. This was next to him, to his skin, and he sent it to me. A gift for my heart, and I am sobbing again.

I know it will be days before I can digest all the meanings, all the depth of this box. The blue fog is gone. I feel worthy of this, of this gift. I do not understand how it happened, but I know that I deserved this, I earned it somehow. I don't know how. I feel so many things. I can't absorb all that is going through my mind, and through my heart, and the tears water my cheeks as I bring the things inside the house, an armful at a time.

I put the music into the CD player, and listen as yes, calming flows through the house and into my heart. I look at the books one by one. I feel the thumbed through pages and marvel at the thought that I am going to read the same words on the same paper, not over an electronic connection, but on paper. I examine the bulbs for evidence of their color or variety and find none, how wonderful! It will be another surprise, for other than knowing what kind of flower; I have no idea what their bloom will bring me. I know only that they will bring me joy and remembrance of this magic day.

The wine is shelved; I can't wait to taste it, but must. The leather bound book goes into my purse, I know it will be with me every day now, a repository for the deepest thoughts I have. It will inspire me; its soft sweet scented presence will draw words from me. The shirt into my room, where I stop and inhale it deeply again, amazed at the emotion it draws. More tears. The gourds go into a basket, and the corn is bound with a cord and hung from the door. The pumpkins sit on the table, awaiting my children and their surprise, they didn't think there would be any this year. Still more tears, I am felled again by the generosity, the significance of these gifts. I wonder if he knows, but I am certain he does. In his heart he knows what this means to me. He knows it is magic, and has saved me this day from despair, from hopelessness, from pain. I feel the joyous tears still in my eyes, and marvel that I have such a friend in my life. He is the true gift, the true magic.

Tonight I sip the wine, delicious on my tongue, and write the words I took notes on in the little leather bound book, and listen to the music, and look at the happy gourds and pumpkins on the table, and relive the magic. The amaryllis is potted in a clay vessel my mother painted, a doubly wonderful addition to my table. The wine is stimulating, like a kiss, and does not fog my head as much as free my thoughts. A friend is magic, a friend I have never touched, never seen, never held, yet he is with me now, and will be as long as the magic lives in my heart.

It will live there always.

Holidays Without Non

This year has been tough.

It started on Thanksgiving, but then, the shock was still fresh. A part of our lives was gone, gone forever, never coming back. We expected it; in some ways we even welcomed it. Deep down inside, all of us hoped it would never happen. We lost our Non.

Non was my great-aunt, the never married matriarch of our family. She had been there for all of us, every holiday, every occasion, had been in our lives every single day of our lives. Those that married into the family soon came to feel that Non had always been a part of their lives too. She was a wonderful lady, with enough love to spread around a hundred families the size of ours. A tiny Italian woman, with huge expressive eyes, a lovely smile, and a great deal of grace, she was eternal, her love unchanging. The love we felt for her was also unchanging, no matter how she aged and ailed and forgot who we were. We were her life, all she had. She was the last of her generation, all her brothers and sisters and cousins passed away before her, some early, some late. Her sister had passed away a little over a year before, and she was the last.

Selfish of us, to miss her. Selfish of me, to wish she were still with us. Non had been very ill for many years. A heart problem, cancer, arthritis, glaucoma, knee replacement, her list of ailments was impressive. She was the Job of the medical world, one thing after another. Through it all, she complained, but I'm sure she was glad to still be around. She knew how much we needed her.

November, a week before Thanksgiving, my mother called me to let me know Non was in bad shape. She had been in a nursing home for over a year, and her eyesight was all but gone. Her body was shutting down, a little at a time, giving way to her eighty-eight years of living and loving. And she did live. I thought it was another false alarm. Non had been at death's door so many times in the past several years and had always managed to come back from it. I suppose I knew that this was the last of those times, that this time she would go through that door and into the heaven she believed in. In the end, she did. She slipped away, unknowing. I didn't go to see her in the hospital; I wanted to remember her the way she had been.

Holidays are hard without her. Every day is hard without Non in the world. Holidays are worse. She occupied the Queen Anne chair in my mother's living room, her walker folded beside the chair, my mother's Jack Russell terrier in her lap. Minnie, the terrier, is a hyperactive bundle of doggie nerves, always has been. Nevertheless, she would sit in Non's lap for as long as an hour, being petted, just being there. Minnie understood what she needed more than we did. We helped her to the table for dinner, raised our voices so she could hear us, and the last couple of holidays, helped her eat her food, which she could no longer see. She took care of us all our lives, we simply did for her what she had done for us. She said she didn't want to be a burden to us anymore. She wanted to go. We told her to stop being silly, that she was no burden, that we didn't mind. For the most part, that was true. Sometimes it was an inconvenience, but compared to what she went through all her life watching over and loving all of us, cutting her meat seemed like such a small thing. Such a small thing compared to the prospect of holidays without Non.

She died 2 days before Thanksgiving. I was one of the pallbearers, to the consternation and dismay of the funeral home directors. She carried me when I was a baby, carried me into church, held my hand going up the steps. It was the very least I could do for her, to help her into the church this last time. Thanksgiving went on as it always did, but the Queen Anne chair was heaped with coats and purses. Nobody wanted to sit in it, except for Minnie. We were still in shock and denial. I almost asked, once, who was going to pick up Non from the home, but caught myself in time. We made it through dinner, but the family left more quickly than usual, going back to where they didn't have to look at that empty chair, or think about who was going to take Non home. She was already home.

Christmas was a little different. We were better adjusted to her absence, but it had sunk in now, and the ache was like a tooth that had been removed. I kept exploring that empty space, over and over, only to find it was still empty. Her pile of presents wasn't there. She never needed any of the presents we gave her anyway, but it was a way to show her that we loved her. Maybe we were trying to tie her to the earth with them. "You haven't gotten enough wear out of that sweater yet, you can't die." It didn't work. There were no sweaters, no vases, no pictures to hang on her walls at the home. She could not take it with her, and ultimately some of the presents that had been given to her found their way back. On the way home from Christmas dinner, it hit me so hard I almost burst into tears. Our first Christmas without Non.

Easter evening is passing now, and it's nearly over. We've made it through. Non loved Easter. She loved the flowers, the colors, the returning warmth. She loved to see the kids dressed up in their finest clothes, and she loved dinner on Easter Sunday. We blessed the bread with holy water, and my mother always made an effort to hit Non with a few drops, just for insurance. We didn't bless the bread this year. Nobody commented on it. We had wedding soup, which Non had made for as many years as we could remember, as long as she was able. It was delicious, tasted almost like hers, but with bigger meatballs. I thought she would have mentioned the size of the meatballs, in jest, but knowing she could have done it a little better. I suppose that was her way of driving us, the best way she knew how. We wanted to please her. I wanted to make her proud of me, though I knew that in a million years, I would never be the cook she was.

People did sit in the Queen Anne chair, though. I suppose in some ways, it is getting easier. We're getting used to her not being there. But we still wish she were with us. She wasn't eternal, but her love is there all the same. That will never leave us.

Drumming

The beat starts tentative. The first touch of a drum is exciting. Very different from other instruments, a drum offers no sheet music or need to read notes from a page. It simply is. You drum. Your heart beats and you follow it. That is the first step. If you are afraid, it doesn't work. You learn this very quickly. If you are not meant to drum, you stop then. If you are brave, you may enter a lifelong journey, marching to your own beat.

The hypnotic quality of drumming is well documented. To listen to drums is to want to dance. The hands dance and you dance with them, with your body or hands or both, with your heart and soul. The best drummers dance with their souls. Technical skill does not matter, for best in music is emotion. Drumming is the most elemental and emotional aspect of music. Drum with your soul or not at all. When skill and emotion mingle, miracles occur.

I've never drummed with sticks. Personally, I could never imagine placing a piece of wood between my hands and the skin of a drum. I have heard heart and magic and wonder from drummers that use sticks, and I admire that magic. My relationship with the drum is too personal, however. I need to touch it, to feel the vibration, to sense the warming of the skin beneath my hands. To feel the flesh of the drum tremble in response to the other drummers playing, the anticipation of the moment when hands will meet that flesh and coax it to life and warmth.

Drumming with others is dancing with them. Less self-conscious, more personal. Dancing your being and your heartbeat with theirs. Sensing the life and rhythm in them through the vibration of their instrument. Magic. The minds of the drummers become meshed. The beat slows and quickens in what seems like an orchestration. It seldom is. The music changes without direction. East becomes west, fire is quenched in water then carried off by wind. It is not uncommon for the song to stop, as surely as if someone had called for the stop. Yet, no one has. Drummers become unified, beating as one.

Drumming for a time leads to an altered mental state. The rhythms of the brain conform to what the ears are hearing, a light trance ensues. Visions may come. Dreams may flash before open eyes. The imagination is fired and what emerges from that kiln can be miraculous indeed. Rhyme and reason, nonsense and prose, careless meandering and hard reality. Power hums in the air. All things are possible.

Tunes without melodies happen. The skin becomes pliant beneath skilled hands. The hands begin to tingle, vibrating along with the drum. Nerve endings sing, and if you strike wrong, there is pain. Most often, the pain is not noticed until much later, when the swelling starts. Like the heart that aches when opened, the hands ache when meeting their destiny. The hands, however, become accustomed to the skin of the drum, while the heart forgets the pain and experiences it anew.

I am relatively new to drumming, having experienced it for the first time less than six months ago. Unsure of this but hoping, I believe that the drum will stay with me for a lifetime. A love that will not abandon nor hurt nor leave, only grow stronger and more passionate as I fix my heart more strongly to the fiber.

Afterword

Thanks for reading.

I hope you enjoyed seeing the world through different eyes.

If I may offer a bit of advice, don't ever be afraid to let people see the world your way. Don't wait too long, and don't worry about what they say, or if they might go running screaming into the street. Share your heart, your words, your vision. That way, you'll never wonder what might have happened if you had not been afraid, or shy, or too uncertain about your ability. You'll know, and sure knowledge is always best.

February 20, 2000
Pittsburgh, PA.